THE CRYSTAL ALLY CARDS ™

The Crystal Path to Self Knowledge

BY

NAISHA AHSIAN

Heaven and Earth
Publishing

East Montpelier, VT

The Crystal Ally Card: The Crystal Path to Self Knowledge
by Naisha Ahsian
Copyright ©1995 by Heaven and Earth Publishing LLC
P.O. Box 249, East Montpelier, VT 05651 USA

Heaven and Earth Publishing
POB 249
East Montpelier, VT 05651
802-476-4775

ISBN 978-0-9621910-1-5
ISBN 0-9621910-1-9

Printed in China

The information contained herein is for educational and/or entertainment purposes only. Neither the author nor the publisher advocates the use of stones as a substitute for medical or psychological care. Appropriate use of the information contained herein is the express responsibility of the reader.

Acknowledgements

Thanks to the Crystal Allies,
TA, Kat, Storm Crow, Eagle Walker,
Aka, Thunder Boy, Rain Woman,
Wolf, Frog, and all
of my spirit allies.

This work is dedicated to my daughter Marie Sierra Hope, who have been my guiding star throughout the birthing of this project.

Many heartfelt thanks to Robert Simmons and Kathy Warner, for their work in bringing Heaven to Earth, and without whom this book could not have become manifest.

Also, to all of those who have guided, taught, helped, hurt, healed, or held me, thank you for the lessons.

Contents

A NOTE ABOUT THE CARDS

When I was first gifted by Spirit with the concept for this book and card deck, my mind was filled with richly colored and powerful images which would incorporate actual stone photography with scenes which would illustrate the stones' gifts. I knew from personal experience that photography could record the energies of gemstones and crystals, because the image it produced was a physical record of light vibrations as they moved through, and emanated from, the stone's body.

But I also knew that this deck was to be more than a photographic representation of stones. I was being guided to create a deck that would lead others into a state of resonance with the Crystal Allies and their energies within the Earth's field. I wished to manifest an *experience* of the stones energy, not simply a representation of their physical beings.

Not being trained in classical art, and knowing that the images must match those that were being gifted to me in inner visions, I asked the Crystal Allies how I could create these energetic representations. The answer I immediately received was, "Create the images on a computer!". This answer made total sense to me, as computers themselves depend upon crystals to function! So I set out on a journey of faith, laying out much of my family's savings in order to purchase the hardware and software necessary to create the images I was seeing in my mind's eye.

The images you see in this deck are the fruit of almost three years of intensive creation and spiritual manifestation. All of the images utilize photographs, either traditional or digital, of actual crystals and stones. Some of these photographs are obvious, being used as the main visual component of the card. Other photographs were used as "texture maps," giving other elements within the image the particular stone's color and texture.

Where a human form was required in order to illustrate a stone's concept, I have used as neutral a form as possible. These forms are meant to suggest human spirit only, and do not represent any particular race or type of person. I have tried to use a balance of male and female figures in the illustrations, reflecting either the predominant stone energy, the elemental energy, or simply to represent human form.

As these images revealed themselves to me and I began to share them with others, I was continually awed by the wonderful reactions that people were having to them. It seemed that the cards were able to create a shift within a person's energetic field, allowing them to sense the gemstone energies more fully. The Crystal Allies had manifested their energies within the images they had revealed to me!

And so, I offer these images to you with the knowledge that they are an energetic doorway– a doorway that opens upon a path to greater self knowledge and connection to personal power– a path to communion with the Crystal Allies!

In Light,
Naisha

PREFACE

A Native American holy man sits beneath the stars and prays for rain to relieve the terrible drought that has endangered his people. Chanting softly, he pierces the skin of his forearm with a flake of chert, allowing drops of his blood to fall upon a small slab of precious turquoise on the Earth in front of him. The stone's spirit, he believes, will carry his offering to the Thunder Beings and persuade them to bring the storms.

An ancient Gypsy woman, arrayed in colorful scarves, leans over a painstakingly fashioned sphere of clear crystal quartz. She peers within the swirls and clouds of it's inclusions, seeking to divine the future fortunes of those who seek her wisdom.

An Aleut hunter sits before his home fire, carefully flaking shards of obsidian off a core to form a spear point. As he works the piece he prays to the spirit of the stone, asking it to protect him from harm as he hunts, and to speak to the spirits of those he kills, telling them of his thanks for their sacrifice.

Crystals and stones have held mystical meaning for humans since before the dawn of history. For millennia tribal shamans and holy people from nearly every culture and race have employed crystals and stones in their healing practices. Throughout history people have worn stones as talismans, and seers have utilized crystals for divination. To the Native European 'Earth Mother' religions of my ancestors, and those of many Native American, African, and Asian tribes, the magical energies of crystals and stones have been powerful allies in spiritual and healing practices. Like herbs, which were used in curing illness, stones were considered to have a spirit or energy within, which could be called upon to aid the healer in his or her work. Stones were prescribed as antidotes, curatives, balancing agents, and as spiritual teachers. In many of these cultures crystals and stones were considered to be living beings.

Over the centuries, we have removed ourselves from the natural world that our ancestors knew so intimately. We have drifted away from our tribal roots, and the sacred knowledge that was held by our elders has nearly been lost. As we stand upon the brink of the New Age, we are turning once more to the ancient source of power that our forbearers honored. We are once again exploring our relationship with the Earth, and with the gifts that she has given to us in the form of crystals and stones.

The Great Earth Mother upon which we live is an incredibly complex entity. She reacts (just as we do) to the other beings around her, such as the sun, moon, and planets. Her children are the four kingdoms of nature, Mineral, Plant, Animal, and Human, all of which interact and depend upon one another for life. Of these children, plants, animals, and humans all depend upon the mineral kingdom as the basis for their life on the planet.

It is the mineral kingdom which makes up the soil of the planet and fills the waters with rich nutrients. It is the mineral kingdom that gives sustenance to the plant kingdom, which in turn sustains the animal and human kingdoms. But the mineral kingdom does much more than simply feed the plants that we eat. Minerals also carry the most important ingredient for life on this planet– energy.

The Earth generates an incredibly powerful energy field that surrounds and permeates everything upon the planet. This energy field acts as the "base note" upon which all life on Earth depends. In states of deep meditation, our own energy field begins to match the vibratory frequency of the Earth's field. In this state of resonance with the planet, we are actually vibrating in harmony with the combined energy fields of each and every one of the minerals and crystals on Earth! Resonating with the Earth's energetic field in this way can open one to an almost unlimited source of energy and spiritual power.

Just as we have different organs within our bodies that perform different functions, the Earth contains many different minerals that vibrate in a rainbow of energetic frequencies. These minerals act as the "organs" of the planet, working in harmony with each other to sustain the energetic field of the Earth. This "energy soup" is the electromagnetic field, or aura, of our planet. Within this aura each type of stone and crystal has a specific frequency of vibration. When we allow our own energy to resonate with the frequency of a particular type of mineral, the resulting vibrational field can initiate in us the experiences of physical and emotional healing, spiritual awakening, and higher states of consciousness.

By entering into resonance with the energy the Earth, you can access and call upon the frequency of any stone on the planet, without the necessity of having a stone or crystal in your hand. This energy is available to you at any moment, anywhere you may be, in unlimited amounts.

I have created *The Crystal Ally Cards* as a way to help you to access and experience these energies, as well as the energies of the elemental forces that surround us. By using the cards in this deck as focusing tools, you can intend resonance with the frequency of energy that the particular stone on the card carries. By using the cards in the layouts outlined within, you can receive messages and guidance for your life from the spirits of the stones themselves.

The crystals and stones that appear on these cards are beings that are willing to aid us in our struggle to return to balance, both with nature and within ourselves. They have come as messengers, teachers and allies in our search for understanding. They are here to help us to reconnect with the primal energies our ancestors communed with, and to assist us in regaining our inheritance as children of the Earth, and of the Light.

There are hundreds of different types of minerals on Earth, and each one of these can be a valuable Ally on the crystal path to self-discovery. Because of the space available, however, I could not include them all and maintain any degree of cohesiveness within this work. The crystals and stone Allies that I have included in this deck represent a wide variety of energetic frequencies and life lessons. I encourage you to use this deck as a "jumping off place" for your own journey into the realm of mineral energies, and to continue your explorations far beyond the range of minerals I have provided within this book.

I hope that by using this book and divination system, you will renew and strengthen your connection with the divine energies of the Earth Mother, and that you will honor yourself and her through your explorations. By honoring her gifts to us, we honor the Mother. By honoring our personal gifts and power, we learn to honor others.

I offer this learning for the highest good of all concerned.

LIGHT

The first spark of consciousness congealed within the infinite mind of the Divine Creator, and it was Light. Every creation that followed, even the creation of matter, has as its foundation that initial spark of consciousness. The energy of Light is the most powerful force one can call upon when seeking healing or spiritual growth, because it is the foundation of all else in our reality.

Humanity has known of the power of spiritual Light energy since before empirical science began. Religious art from many different cultures, including the cave paintings of stone age humans, depict their highest spiritual teachers with halos or crowns of light around their heads. Spiritual texts throughout history have spoken of encounters with beings of Light, angels, and the Light of God. Ancient and modern healers describe the ability to perceive Light energy passing through their hands and into their patients, healing imbalances and dis-ease on the deepest levels.

Light is defined by science as the full spectrum of electromagnetic radiation. A very small part of this spectrum, about 1/100 of the measurable frequencies, is visible to us as light and color. The rest of the measurable light spectrum includes radio waves, microwaves, ultraviolet and infrared waves, and hundreds of other frequencies of energy that affect matter down to the smallest particles.

The range of frequencies that we call "spiritual Light" energy are not measurable using our current scientific equipment and knowledge. These frequencies include the scientific definition of light, but extend far beyond their limited scope, to include particles and waves that are currently not detectable to our instrumentation. These frequencies of energy are perceptible, however, through the use of our extrasensory perceptions, or "psychic" abilities. Spiritual seekers have been utilizing these frequencies of Light for healing, self-exploration, and spiritual growth for millennia.

The aura or energy field that surrounds all matter is one such set of frequencies that are not currently perceptible to mainstream science. Auras are a palpable energy, however, and can be felt by those who have had minimal training in the use of the psychic senses.

In humans, this field of Light energy reflects one's health, experiences, and emotions, by exhibiting colors and vibrations which relate to the energy centers of the body.

Can it be that there is another set of frequencies in the light spectrum which are of a faster vibration than those included in the scientific definition of light? Can there be light frequencies that travel faster than our instruments can detect, and so exist beyond the physical realm? Can these frequencies of light be influenced by human thought and intent?

Until recently, science would have answered with a resounding NO! Yet our own empirical science may now be catching up with the most primitive stone age shaman. Quantum physicists have begun to theorize that there is one force in the universe which contains and creates all others, a force from which all others spring. In quantum physics this primal force is the "unified theory", and it remains an elusive mystery. In metaphysics, it is called the Divine Creative Force, and it is perceptible to each and every one of us, within and around every particle of matter in our reality, as spiritual Light frequencies.

Just as the visible aspect of Light energy is only a very limited range of frequencies in the full spectrum of Light, the visible part of you, your physical body, is composed of a very limited range of frequencies in the total vibration of your full conscious being. Physical matter is composed of those particles which are vibrating at so slow a frequency that they coalesce into larger particles and become matter. Your physical body, then, is simply one part of your own conscious energy existing at a lower frequency of vibration than the non-physical aspects of your conscious self.

Most of your total conscious being is vibrating at rates too fast to be experienced by your physical body. Your mind, for instance, experiences thoughts every moment of every day, yet these thoughts cannot be measured or tracked by any instrument our science currently possesses. Your mind itself, consciousness, cannot be physically touched; yet there is no question that we are sentient beings. The energy of consciousness is part of the spiritual Light range of frequencies that you can learn to perceive through practicing basic meditation and awareness exercises.

These frequencies of Light can also be experienced and sensed by learning to utilize those parts of your total being that are vibrating at a similarly high rate. For instance, when you learn to experience the feel of your own aura, you can then utilize your aura to detect similar vibrations in other beings. This ability to sense and experience the energies of other physical bodies is called *resonance*. The ability to consciously resonate with other beings is a vital skill in healing and psychic work. It is also extremely valuable when working with stones and crystals.

Just as our physical self is only the "visible" range of our own total energy systems, so too are crystals and stones the "visible" manifestations of their total energies. When you resonate with these beings, you are using Light energy to communicate and exchange information, knowledge and thoughts, with the consciousness of the stone.

When you enter into resonance with a crystal or stone, the part of your energy which vibrates at the resonant level becomes amplified and strengthened. The resulting vibrations can cause changes in the emotional, spiritual and physical aspects of your experience. The practice of consciously engaging the energies of a stone or stones to affect changes in the physical, emotional or spiritual bodies, is called *Crystal Resonance Therapy* ™.

Part of the visible light spectrum is composed of energetic frequencies that we perceive with our eyes as the spectrum of color. Part of our own energy frequencies can also be perceived on the psychic level as "etheric" color. These etheric colors are part of the spectrum of spiritual Light that makes up our total being– physical and non-physical. These frequencies of Light are manifested in our physical bodies within our chakras, or energy centers.

Chakras are vortexes of energy that supply our body with the full spectrum of energy that it needs in order to maintain physicality. Each of the chakras in our body is keyed to a specific frequency, or wavelength, of energy. There are seven major chakras in the physical body, and hundreds of minor chakras in our physical and energetic fields. There are also etheric chakras within our energy field that are our source for receiving spiritual Light from the non-physical aspects of our total selves. The seven major chakras of the physical body are each linked to a color in the spectrum of visible (physical) light.

The first chakra is located at the base of the spine, and it's color is red. The second, or navel chakra, is located just below the bellybutton, and it's color is orange. The third, or solar plexus chakra, is located about two inches above the navel, and it's color is yellow. The fourth chakra, or heart chakra, is located just above and between the nipples, and is green. The fifth chakra, also called the throat chakra, is located at the base of the throat in the hollow of the collar bone, and it is blue in color. The sixth chakra, or third eye, is located above and between the eyebrows, and is indigo. The seventh, or crown chakra, is located at the crown of the skull, and is violet in color. By using the appropriate color on a chakra, one can strengthen and balance it.

The colors of these chakras are not readily apparent to most people with the naked eye. They are perceptible, however, through the use of extrasensory perception. When working with crystals and stones you will notice that often the color of a stone will be a clue as to the frequency of it's vibration, and the chakra with which it will resonate most strongly. A stone may be effective on more than one chakra, however, so use the color of the stone as an initial guide only, until you are more familiar with it's energy and frequency of resonance.

Non-visible frequencies of Light energy are also carried by the internal molecular structure of crystals and stones. In addition to a color frequency, a stone can also carry the frequencies of the stone's particular mineral species, the Earth's total energy field, and the elemental force with which the stone resonates. All of these energies combine to form the aura of the stone. When resonating with the aura of a crystal you can access any of the particular frequencies of energy that it carries.

The planet upon which we live consists of every type of stone and crystal that will ever be found on Earth. By attuning to resonance with the energy field of the Earth, you can access the frequency of any stone you choose. Just imagine the vast amounts of energy that are available to the Lightworker every day through attuning to the aura of the planet!

But the planet itself is not the only source of energy available to the Lightworker. There exists, too, a greater consciousness that feeds all physicality. I call this energy "The Great Earth Mother"; reflecting the ability of this consciousness to provide for, and nurture, all beings on the Earth plane.

The Great Earth Mother is the combined consciousness of all physicality. This consciousness is not only that of the physical planet, but also every creature and being that inhabits the planet. Some of her frequencies are visible and palpable to us in the physical world, and some are more difficult to perceive. The "physical" frequencies of her energy manifest as the natural elemental forces of Earth, Water, Fire, and Wind. These elements are incredible sources of power an energy for the Lightworker in the New Age.

Each of the elemental forces of nature is necessary to maintain the well being of every creature on the planet. Each of these forces represent a set of energetic frequencies, without which the total being of the Great Earth Mother could not sustain itself. As children of the Great Earth Mother, we each carry aspects of these vital elemental energies within us. When we resonate with the conscious Light of these elements we strengthen our own vital forces. In turn, this resonance also allows us to share our energy and love with the Great Earth Mother.

We have come to Earth in this lifetime in order to be emissaries of Light in the physical world. We have come to return the balance between humanity and nature, and to once again take our place as children of The Great Earth Mother and the Divine Creator. Crystals and stones are a wonderful reminder of how Light manifests as matter. As you hold in your hand the purity and clarity of a quartz crystal, you come to understand the idea that physicality is only one part of Spirit. We can all become crystals of Light upon Earth, by resonating with the gifts of manifest Light that we have been given in the forms of the mineral kingdom and the elemental forces.

The experience of Light through resonance with crystals and stones, elemental energies, and your own higher self, connects you to the source of all that is. Through these experiences you will come to know your own special place in the world, and the strength of your own personal power. The Crystal Allies, Elemental Allies, and your own personal guides are waiting to take you beyond the illusion of form, and into the great web of Light that binds all things together in the mind of the Divine Creator. Open yourself now to the energies that surround you, and take your place in the Light!

ᴇARTH MAGIC

Within our bodies and beings are billions of cells, zillions of molecules, and countless atomic and sub-atomic particles. Each of these parts carries its own vibration, specific to itself. Imagine the number of specific vibrations that combine to create the vibration in the community of a molecule. Now imagine the number of molecules that must exist in energetic harmony in order to create the being and vibration of just one of the cells in your fingernail or eye. Imagine the incredible harmony and energy of these cells coming together to form the components of your little finger or toe.

All of this matter is vibrating at an incredible rate, all in concert and harmony with the components of itself and those particles that surround it. The energy of all of these sub-atomic particles vibrating in harmony creates our bodies and our energetic field, or aura.

The riot of diversity that is our body and energy field is formed from the same basic building blocks as everything else on the planet—molecules of carbon, silica, water, and iron, just to name a few. A molecule of the hemoglobin in your blood is incredibly similar to a molecule of chlorophyll, the lifeblood of the plant world.

The molecules in our bodies are communities of atoms and sub-atomic particles vibrating together in order to experience the realm of physicality. The community of silica molecules that nourish our bodies carries the same vibration as those that form under the planet's surface as quartz crystals. The iron molecules in our bodies are essentially the same as those that form iron ore in the Earth. It is the same as the iron that flows through the veins of the goldenrod plant on the side of the road or the hummingbird or butterfly in your garden.

When this grand orchestra of vibration misses a note somewhere in the system, the result is discord throughout the total system. Cells that are no longer vibrating in unison begin to interfere with each others' functions, making health (unity of vibration) disappear, and dis-ease (discord) flourish.

We can see how this affects us on a macrocosmic scale right now, reflected in the havoc that humans are creating in our world. Humans have separated themselves from their environment, and in so doing, they have caused discord within the body of the Great Earth Mother (all creation unified). This discord has created a breakdown in the system, causing even more discord, which has resulted in our polluting and

damaging the world in which we live. We are acting very much like
cancer cells within a body– causing the vibration of those around us to
become discordant, until the body is so diseased it must perish.

We have all chosen to incarnate on Earth at this time of change in
order to bring a remembrance of harmony to humanity. The cancer that
humanity's mayhem has created on the planet can only be healed by
teaching those who are out of tune with the great song of life to once
again move into measure with the natural song of creation. We have
come to heal our own discord; and in so doing, heal the total being of
the Great Earth Mother– planet, plant, animal, human, and spirit.

It is not as bleak as it may sound. By and large, the great orchestra
of vibration that is created and carried by the planet, animals, and
plants is being played as well as ever. But our own vibration has
become increasingly damaging to the macrocosm of vibration in which
we live. How can we bring ourselves back into harmony with the
vibration of creation around us? By entering into resonance with that
natural vibration, and integrating it's energy into our own energetic fields
and physical bodies.

There are many tools to aid us in coming back into resonance with
the natural harmony around us. When we sit quietly within the energetic
soup of nature and allow ourselves to begin to resonate with the natural
energy that surrounds us, our individual communities of protons and
neutrons, atoms and molecules, compounds and cells, begin to find
alignment and harmony with those particles of similar vibration that are
singing around us.

The vibration of silica that hums in our tissues begins to vibrate with
the song of the quartz crystals that are growing beneath the surface of
the planet, the molecules of silica in the grains of sand on a beach, and
the silica that is nourishing the grass upon which we sit. The silica
within us *remembers* it's part of the harmony of nature. Every element,
compound, and energetic community that makes up our body begins to
find it's natural tone again. The more often we "tune in" to nature, the
more "in tune" we become! Our bodies can become healthier, our minds
clearer, and our spirits more present and active in our bodies.

This brings us to crystals and minerals. Every type of crystal or
mineral contains molecules of compounds and elements that vibrate in
concert with one another. These stones carry a specific note, or set of
notes in the song of energy that is made by the Earth. These beings
are"programmed" with a certain frequency that is a part of the total
energetic field of the planet.

When we bring a crystal or stone into our own energetic field and
begin to resonate with it, those parts of us that recognize that vibration
will begin to change their frequency to match that of the mineral. This

creates shifts within our aura. We perceive these shifts as emotions, sensations and spiritual experiences of connecting with a universal whole. Because different crystals and stones "sing" to different aspects of our being, we can utilize their frequencies as allies in our path to regain harmony with the Great Earth Mother (all creation in Unity).

There are other forces on the planet that can be accessed on an energetic level as well. These energies are referred to as the elemental forces. These are the basic patterns of energy movement on the planet; and they have great influence over the way that we live and experience our lives.

The first of these elemental forces is one that we have already been discussing, that of the planet and the mineral kingdom. This force pertains more to the energies generated by the planet than it's actual composition. The forces of gravity and the earth's magnetic field permeate every bit of matter on the planet. It is a vast resource for the Lightworker to access and utilize in her energetic work. This element has influence over the physicality of our lives, creations and issues of being in a physical body. The Earth, being the "bones" of the Great Earth Mother, represents the most stable and physical aspects of our lives. The subtle energies of the earth element are the base notes for the vibrations of our Earthstar and first chakras. When we are connected with the Earth and it's energies, we are more capable of functioning on a daily basis in our lives.

The second of these natural elemental forces is the energy of Fire. This energy is the life force of Earth, and it's power is represented by the molten core of the planet. It is also represented by lightning, which can create physical fire on the planet's surface. This fire is an incredible force of change and purification. Though leaving destruction in it's wake, it also creates space for growth as it enriches the earth, so that new creations can grow and new manifestations can thrive. It clears the old and unproductive aspects from the Earth and from our lives, allowing new experiences and creations to take root. This element rules the second and third chakras of our energetic systems. These chakras are the centers of creation, manifestation, sexuality and the will. Invoking the energy of Fire can be a powerful way to cleanse stagnant energies that are in need of total transformation.

The third elemental force is that of Water. Water is one of the crucial materials that our bodies need to sustain life. It is "liquid air", the blood of the Earth, and a powerful source of energy for the cleansing of the heart and emotions. Water is yielding and receptive, yet it can wear down mountains if given time. From this element we learn release, constancy, joy, and the way of water– going with the flow. The element of water rules the heart and throat chakras, the home of emotions and sound. By utilizing water energy one can clear old emotional patterns, learn to express oneself more fully, and sooth and heal our emotional wounds.

The fourth elemental force is Wind. This element represents the energy of the mind. It is the most yielding and elusive element, and yet it's power surrounds us each moment in our breath, in the breeze and in our thoughts. Wind is the energy of Spirit. It is the means by which our spirits can travel great distances or soar to new heights. Wind energy gives us wings to explore and experience things of which we earthbound creatures could not otherwise conceive of. It is a reminder of our original state; when we existed as pure energy, without the density of a physical body. The wind element governs the third eye and crown chakras. This element's power brings us visions and communications from spirit.

When all of these elemental forces combine, we experience the force of Storm. This is the most sacred and purifying force that we can invoke, as it cleanses and recharges every chakra and energy system in our body. Have you ever noticed the purifying effects of a storm after a stagnant, hot summer day? Or the beauty and joy of a white blanket of snow on the ground after a "Nor'easter"? This feeling of having been deeply cleansed and revitalized is no accident. Our bodies respond to the excited energies, or "song" of the storm as our molecules and atoms react to the negative ions that Storm generates. The crackle of lightening, the howl of the wind, and the torrent of rain upon the Earth – this is the instant of total unity. It is destruction and creation in one moment.

Just as every element within us responds to the song of nature when we quiet ourselves to hear it, the atoms and molecules that make up our physical bodies respond to the frequencies that form the elemental forces. When we tune in to the element of water, every molecule of water and every atom of hydrogen and oxygen within our system, begins to vibrate with that native energy. When we resonate with the energy of fire, every atom of carbon and every spark of electrical energy within our nervous system reacts in kind. Each time we invoke the energy of Wind, our spirits and etheric energies vibrate in harmony with the breath of the Great Earth Mother.

Our bodies and energies are constantly resonating with some or all of these aspects. We are generally unconscious of the influence and power that these elemental forces hold over us. When we move into harmony with theses forces and learn to invoke their powers, we not only gain greater personal strength and understanding, but we also strengthen the planet and all other inhabitants of the spaceship Earth. When we learn to invoke, utilize and honor these forces, both within ourselves and within their outward reflections in the world, a whole new reality opens to us, precluding the concept of separation from the Earth or each other.

In the Crystal Ally Cards, each crystal belongs to an elemental family. When using the cards, not only can the individual stone's energies be taken into account, but also the patterns that form from the elemental families that the stones inhabit. There are many layers of meaning within the card layouts that will take you far beyond the metaphysical properties of the stones themselves.

I hope as you begin to use the cards you will also take some time to do the meditations and exercises included in the book. These meditations and exercises will aid you in beginning to attune to the incredible store of energies that are available for you to utilize in your spiritual and personal work.

I offer this creation to you in the hope that it may help you to discover your own unique sounding in the symphony of creation.

INTRODUCTION TO
CRYSTAL RESONANCE THERAPY

Crystal– *Chem.., Mineral,* 1. a solid having a characteristic internal structure and enclosed by symmetrically arranged plane surfaces, intersecting at definite and characteristic angles. 2. Resembling crystal; clear or transparent.[1]

Resonance– *Physics,* 1. the state of a system in which an abnormally large vibration is produced in response to an external stimulus, occurring when the frequency of the stimulus is the same, or nearly the same, as a natural vibration of the system.[2]

Therapy– 1. the application of treatment in order to affect change or improvement in a system.

Crystal Resonance Therapy™– 1. the application of crystals and stones to a system, in order to create a state of resonance, to affect change or improvement in that system. 2. The use of specific techniques in order to create a state of resonance, with varying frequencies of Light energy, within the molecular structure of a human, for the purpose of spiritual growth and self-healing.

   In looking at the above definitions for Crystal Resonance Therapy™ there are two distinct meanings that make themselves apparent. The first definition describes Crystal Resonance Therapy™ (CRT) as the practice of using crystals and stones to create a vibrational field which induces a state of resonance, and affects healing, in a person or system. This is the definition of CRT that most closely resembles the practice of 'crystal healing'. This aspect of CRT involves placing stones or crystals upon the body and passing an energetic vibration through

1. Random House College Dictionary
2. Same

them in order to affect change in the vibrational rate of the human energy field.

The practice of laying on of stones is an ancient one; and there has been much written about the methods one can use in laying stones on the body to facilitate healing. CRT utilizes laying on of stones as one of it's main healing practices. But CRT moves beyond the physical practice of the laying on of stones, and into the powerful realm of conscious vibration. By practicing resonance with a variety of high frequency energies, the Crystal Resonance Therapist is able to act as a transmitter and amplifier of energetic fields. This enables the practitioner to utilize much more powerful vibrations than the laying on of stones alone can generate.

It is through the personal practice of "conscious resonance" that one learns to establish and transmit these frequencies of energy. Conscious resonance is a meditative practice that enables a person to adjust her vibratory frequency, in order to resonate with various frequencies of Light energy. The most powerful form of conscious resonance that is practiced in CRT is called Crystal Resonance.

Crystal resonance is a state of vibration in which the practitioner resonates on a cellular level with specific frequencies of Light that are similar to those carried by the mineral kingdom. This is done in order to clear and activate the energetic and physical body of the practitioner. At this level of vibration, the practitioner is able to experience and amplify Light energy through her physical body in the same way that a quartz crystal does. In this way, the practitioner becomes, in a sense, a human crystal.

This practice illustrates the second definition of Crystal Resonance Therapy™, which is the experience of resonance with Light energies in order to establish a clear, crystalline vibration for the purpose of spiritual growth and healing.

Through the practice of conscious resonance, one learns to experience and transmit other vibrational fields as well. One can, through the practice of CRT, learn to match one's own vibratory field to that of any crystal or stone, elemental force, or other source of spiritual light energy. Through this practice, the Crystal Resonance Therapist is able to transmit amplified energy frequencies through his/her own energetic field in order to create change in the resonant field of others.

So, the term Crystal Resonance Therapy™ indicates the practice of very specific modalities of healing that go beyond the practice of laying on of stones. You cannot be a Crystal Resonance Therapist only by practicing the laying on of stones. There is a large field of knowledge that one must explore and integrate in order to practice CRT. The modality of laying on of stones is just one part of that total system.

The primary element of Crystal Resonance Therapy™ is the personal practice of conscious resonance, and especially Crystal Resonance. Once you begin practicing the exercises and meditations of Crystal Resonance, you naturally begin to heal yourself and others on an energetic level, simply by changing the level of vibration that you emit!

As the great teacher Yashua said, "Physician, heal thyself." This powerful statement illustrates the necessity of healing the self first, so that the knowledge and wisdom that you gain in your own healing process can then be applied in facilitating others in their healing journeys.

When we incarnate into an earthly lifetime, we choose a set of personal challenges that will act as our teachers in the lessons we have chosen to explore. It is by moving through these challenges that we gather our personal power and develop our inner clarity. When these challenges have been incorporated and overcome, they are transformed into gifts which the healer can then utilize and share with others.

Early levels of CRT training focus upon healing and integrating those aspects of one's life that are in need of transformation. Once one has begun to clear one's own energetic patterns, one is then able to perceive more clearly and accurately the energetic imbalances in others. This makes one much more effective when attempting to create resonant vibration for the purpose of healing another.

Aside from the practice of conscious resonance, crystals and stones are our most valuable help-mates in all levels of Crystal Resonance Therapy and practice. The ability of crystals and stones to initiate and hold a particular vibrational field is extremely valuable in teaching their human counterpart to do the same. By learning to resonate with the vibrations of different crystals and stones, we expand our own repertoire of healing vibrations, which we can then transmit to others.

A Crystal Resonance Therapist honors crystals and stones as valuable teachers and allies in the effort to clarify one's own energy field, so that one may become a human crystal of Light upon the new planet Earth.

CONSCIOUS ALLIES

Crystals and stones are conscious beings, learning and growing spiritually just as we do. But they do not experience existence in the same way humans do. Crystals and stones experience their existence as a constant state of conscious resonance with fields of physical and spiritual vibration.

Unlike humans, the Crystal Allies have never experienced a sense of separation between their physical and non-physical selves. Their consciousness is able to experience both physicality and communion with Spirit simultaneously. Even as a crystal is birthed from the heat and gasses of creation, it's physical existence is only a recording device for it's spiritual consciousness. It exists sometimes, for millions of years in a state of communion with vibration and consciousness. Even as a stone's body is transformed to sand by the movement of the tides, it experiences this vibrational communion, with each particle of sand vibrating with the whole that it had been.

This is one of the most valuable lessons we can learn from the mineral kingdom. Through the constant state of conscious resonance with Light energy, we too can become physical extensions of our total conscious being. As we practice the meditations and states of resonance in CRT, we are able to become more clear and more capable of holding this Light vibration. We truly will become human crystals of Light.

At the dawning of the age of Light, many stones are choosing to be birthed onto the planet surface in order to learn about the frequencies of Light energy that are now being initiated within humanity. They have also come to teach us how to hold a field of conscious resonance with the Light. In this way, humanity is being awakened to the mineral kingdom within and the powerful potential of our evolution into human Light beings.

By choosing to come to the surface of the planet and interact with other beings, stones are able to learn much that will further their spiritual evolution, just as we learn much from them that will further the spiritual growth of humanity. When a stone comes in contact with another being, it has the opportunity to learn by experiencing resonance with that being's vibration. By resonating at levels that it has not previously experienced, the stone learns about carrying an expanded range of energies.

The vibrations that are experienced by a crystal's work with other beings is recorded within the stone's structure as pure information. Many people who have been working with stones have uncovered "recorded" information within the stone's molecular structure. Much of this information was recorded during the Atlantean period, the last historic period in which humankind worked as closely with the mineral kingdom as we are doing today.

But this information is not recorded only within the molecular structure of individual stones. Indeed, these stones are only the fore-runners, or information gatherers, of the mineral world. The experiences that they gather are transmitted to every other stone of it's vibrational "family" as well.

THE GREAT LIBRARY

All stones vibrate within a similar range of frequencies. Stones of a particular type will share a set of vibrational frequencies, while each has a 'personal' energetic signature that reflects it's conscious energy. For instance, all quartz carries a specific set of vibrations. Amethyst, as a variety of quartz, will combine the quartz frequency with the frequency of Iron, which gives it it's beautiful color. An individual amethyst crystal will carry these vibrations, plus the individual vibrations of it's personal soul consciousness and the vibration that is created by the particular way it's own physical body carries all of these vibrations together.

These vibrations are carried within the spectrum of energy which is the Earth's energetic field. As we move through our day, we are constantly moving through this vibrant field of resonant stone energies. This field acts like a giant radio system. All beings of a certain frequency are able to "broadcast" and receive information along that frequency. So, the information that a stone gains in working with a human is transmitted to, and recorded by, *all of the others stones of that type*– whether they are within the Earth or on it's surface!

This information is carried by the common resonant fields of the stones, and is recorded within their molecular structures as energetic patterns. Now that humanity has begun working with crystals and stones in ever increasing numbers again, this constant information transmission has begun to create a rich and diverse library of experience that is being recorded by the mineral kingdom.

The advanced Crystal Resonance Therapist is able to access this informational storehouse and gain knowledge on how stones have been used on the planet, and on what the results of that use were. Imagine having this store of information available to you! Through conscious resonance, you would be able to utilize the modality of laying on of stones to it's utmost potential, having first hand information on the best and most effective way of using a particular stone in any given situation.

In CRT, the practitioner also learns how to access the total energetic field of any type of stone from within the electromagnetic field of the Earth, and then to apply that immensely powerful field of resonance in a healing situation. This ability greatly enhances the efficacy of gemstone healing. Instead of relying on the energetic capacity of a single stone, the CRT practitioner is able to use that stone and her own energetic field, as a channel for the healing vibration of all of that stone's vibrational family. The advanced practitioner can also access the energies of any stone family through the Earth's energetic field, and apply that energetic frequency without the necessity of having a stone's body present.

Humans are quickly evolving to a point where we will be able to share information and learning with each other as rapidly as the mineral kingdom can. Indeed, we carry the mineral kingdom around within us in the elements and compounds that our bodies utilize for survival. The silica, out of which every cell in your body is built, carries the same energetic frequencies as a quartz crystal. With conscious resonance, the practitioner could access the informational hologram of every quartz crystal on the planet through the vibration of cellular silica! Accessing this immense store of knowledge will be increasingly possible as we evolve and begin to resonate with the frequencies of the crystals within us.

This is why the spiritual practices of CRT are vitally important. In practicing conscious resonance with the higher forces of the planet and the Universe, we are able to clarify and transform our personal energy field. When we have reached a state of resonant clarity, we are able to then access much more information through our own physical bodies than we ever thought possible before! We each can become transmitters and receivers of information, which we will control through the practice of conscious resonance on a cellular level.

RECOVERING THE TOTAL SELF

The practice of conscious resonance in order to experience the 'crystalline vibration' is one of the core practices of CRT. Through the use of meditative practices,vocal toning and visualization, a field of resonance is created within the physical and energetic body, facilitating the release of energetic blockages and patterns that no longer serve the individual. In clearing the energetic field the practitioner raises the energetic frequency at which she normally vibrates (her "static" vibratory field).

As we go through our life times in the physical realm, we have gathered and stored the energetic imprints of all of our experiences within the crystalline structure of our cells; most especially, within the DNA. Over time, these recorded imprints come to act as energetic filters which affect the way in which energy moves within and through us to create our experiences. The practice of CRT often brings these imprints to the surface by 'shaking them loose' with vibration, and releasing them to the conscious mind to be processed and integrated. One of the side effects of deep conscious resonance is that we begin to clear blockages not only from this lifetime, but from all of our alternate life times as well. This creates deep healing in the current lifetime as the energetic filters that create our reality are cleansed and cleared of debris.

The practice of clearing all energetic imprints from one's vibrational field is called *Energetic Neoteny*. Neoteny is a zoological term which means reaching adulthood in the larval state, or retaining larval characteristics into maturity. Energetic Neoteny is the process of reaching energetic maturity while still in the physical (larval) state.This process can also be called 'becoming pre-born'.

Becoming pre-born is a process through which a person can attain a state of conscious resonance which is not clogged by past experiences-not even the birth experience. This level of resonance gives one access to the higher levels of awareness and understanding that we exist in outside of physicality. By practicing Energetic Neoteny and clearing the filters and blockages within your energetic systems, you will naturally begin vibrating at higher and higher static frequencies. This speeds the process of personal and planetary evolution.

The recovery of information, clearing of the energetic systems, and establishment of a higher vibration within the human crystal creates profound changes in one's life. Just as a wind will blow aside a curtain, the practice of conscious resonance will clear the energetic veils from your higher eyes, revealing your total self to you. But it is not only the personal level that is transformed by this inner work. The experience and transmission of higher vibrational fields sets a larger plan into motion, a plan that has been written within us for millennia.

PLANETARY HEALING

Just as crystals and stones affect change in your energetic systems, because of their higher vibrational rates – so, too, will you begin affecting others with your own higher energies. This makes you a healer in a much larger sense. Not only are you able to affect the energy fields of others through conscious resonance, but you will also be affecting the total energy field of the planet, creating a ripple of higher energy within the energetic field of the Earth. As more and more individuals practice conscious resonance with higher frequencies of Light, the resulting vibration will create a resonant field on the planet that will affect the energetic fields of all beings on Earth.

The theory of resonance states that a system, when it comes into contact with a strong field of vibration, must change it's own vibration in order to become resonant with the stronger vibration. *This is a law of physics.* When we have created a field of conscious resonance of a strong enough vibration upon the planet, all beings that come into contact with that energetic field *must change their vibration to come into resonance.* Since this vibration will be carried through the Earth's electromagnetic field, this means that every being upon the planet will be affected by this higher conscious vibration.

This is our task in the age of Light!

When we have established this field of resonance on the planet, we will initiate the evolution of humanity into a higher spiritual state. The age of Light will fully dawn, and we will begin to manifest a higher civilization upon the planet.

The practice of Crystal Resonance Therapy is one very powerful path we can walk toward this new beginning. As both a personal spiritual practice and a powerful healing modality, CRT will enable us to collectively change the total energetic field of the planet as we change and improve our own lives.

THE EMERGING HUMAN

The role of the Crystal Resonance Therapist, and all of us in this New Age, is to facilitate the energetic and physical evolution of humanity. It is through a concerted effort at higher resonance that we will all grow in understanding and spiritual power. As our vibratory rate increases and the old forms are shaken loose and purified, we will experience the rapid transformation of all of our social, governmental and spiritual institutions.

Within the cellular and sub-atomic structure of our physical beings, there is a beautiful blueprint for the coming evolution of humanity. This blueprint indicates the physical and energetic transformation that humanity will be undergoing in the coming years, as our conscious efforts to raise the vibration of physicality bear fruit.

This plan outlines our evolution into human light beings. This evolution will occur on a physical as well as spiritual level. As we raise our static vibratory rate, we unlock aspects within our genetic makeup that have been dormant for millennia. Our increased ability to access information through vibration will allow us to communicate telepathically. We will be able to affect our physical form through conscious resonance, and will change our physical form to resonate with high frequency Light energy.

As this new understanding dawns, we will also bring forth new concepts for government and life upon the planet. The old forms and institutions will no longer be able to contain the higher vibration that we will be manifesting through the Earth's magnetic field. This will cause a brief period of upheaval as new forms take root.

Our evolution into human Light beings will not be the end to all problems as we know them; but it will be the beginning of true solutions to some of the difficulties we presently face. The healing of our bodies and the planet, food and housing for every person, the end of war and competitive ego-based governmental institutions, and the opportunity for each of us to contribute and explore our own potential, will be some of the benefits we will gain from raising our combined vibration. There is no reason we cannot do all of this and more in the coming times.

As we begin to access our own cellular storehouse of information, we will be able to design new forms that will fit the energetic pattern we are now creating. To do this, we must begin to move away from our "new form–old vibration" creations, and birth that which is truly an expression of our new level of conscious resonance with the Light.

The practice of Crystal Resonance Therapy will aid this goal by creating a group of consciously resonating practitioners throughout the world, creating a field of vibration that will aid all of us in our own personal and collective evolutionary endeavors.

IN CONCLUSION

Because of space and time limitations, this chapter contains only a very brief overview of the practice of Crystal Resonance Therapy™. The complete exploration of the theory and practice of CRT will be outlined in my next book, *Crystal Resonance Therapy™: Becoming the Human Crystal* .

If you would like further information on CRT practice and training, please write to: Lightworks Institute, P.O.Box 54, Marshfield, VT 05658.

CONSULTING THE CRYSTAL ALLIES

The Crystal Ally Cards were created so that you could learn about the properties of gemstones and crystals and apply that understanding to situations in your own life. How can a card convey the energy of a stone? The Earth upon which we stand contains all of the stones and crystals there will ever be. Within her energetic field, there are the frequencies of thousands of different types of minerals. By meditating upon the Crystal Ally Cards that you receive in your layout, you are using your own thought and intention to connect with the frequency of that mineral in the Earth's energetic field.

Each crystal and stone acts as a solidified frequency of energy. All of these frequencies together create the 'aura' of the Earth Mother. When we hold a stone or access it's energy through the cards, we begin to resonate, or vibrate, with the frequency of energy that the particular crystal represents. Our energetic systems reflect the frequency of the stone and create the experience of an emotion or state of consciousness. These impressions can be extremely useful in meditation, vibrational healing, and in divining the dominant patterns in our lives.

And so, I refer to the crystals and stones in this deck as the Crystal Allies. An ally is someone with whom you connect in a personal relationship, such as a friendship or a partnership. When honored, the wisdom, beauty and power of crystals and stone beings make for powerful allies in our search for self understanding. By honoring the insight that these beings can give us, we are honoring the Earth Mother in all of her beauty and power.

GETTING STARTED

To begin consulting your Crystal Allies, find an area that is large enough for you to spread the cards out in a fan shape in front of you. You will also need room in which to place the cards in the layout you choose. A large table or a clear area on the floor are ideal.
It may also be helpful for you to light a candle and play music, in order to enhance the meditative atmosphere.

Remember, what you are really doing is preparing to access part of the Earth's energy field. Approach her with respect and good intent.

Shuffle the cards, allowing some of them to reverse so that they are upside down. When you feel that they are shuffled completely, spread them out in a fan in front of you, allowing the edge of each card to show. Take several long, deep breaths to signal to your body and mind that it is time to relax and focus.

Think about the issue or issues that you wish to explore. Clearly formulate a question or thought in your mind. As you hold this question, place your non-dominant hand about two inches above the cards. Allow your hand to begin to move slowly over the top of the cards. As you pass your hand over the surface of the cards, you may experience a slight tingling sensation, heat, or a muscle twitch. These are indications that you should choose a specific card. When you are drawn to choose a card, take it out and place it in the proper position according to the layout you have chosen. When you have chosen all of the cards for your layout, gather the remaining cards and set them aside. Then follow the process for the interpretation of the cards in the layout.

If you find that any card is unclear in a layout, you can choose a card from the remaining pile to clarify or add to it's meaning. The crystals that appear in your layout are indicating the most dominant forces or energetic frequencies that are involved in the situation you are asking about. If you ask for clarification, it will always be provided.

If you come across a particular crystal whose spirit speaks to you strongly, you can utilize that card as a focus of meditation, drawing it's energy into your own energetic system. You may also carry any card with you throughout the day in order to remind you of it's message.

REVERSED CARDS

The advent of a reversed card in the Crystal Ally Cards is different than many decks that you may have used. There is no separate meaning for a card that is reversed, but a reversal does indicate a deeper meaning in your reading. When a card appears in the reversed position in a layout, it signals an aspect of the current situation that you may be having the most difficulty with. Consequently, it is the aspect that holds the deepest lesson for you.

A reversed card can also indicate the area of blockage in the situation. Either the meaning of the card itself, the position that the card occupies in the layout, or a combination of both, will indicate where the heart or crux of the issue lies.

Reversed cards do not have a negative connotation. They are simply a way for your guides to underscore a certain aspect of your reading. It is in this way that the Crystal Allies provide deeper layers of meaning to your reading. If you should do a layout in which most or all of the cards are in the reverse position, it is an indication that the Crystal Allies are giving you a strong message. The question that you are asking may be particularly important to your personal evolution or life path. It is best to pay particular attention to these types of messages.

Always feel free to do your reading again if you like! Don't forget, however, that taking action in the physical world is worth a lifetime of getting advice from the non-physical world. We are here to do and to learn. Applying the information that the cards give you is a positive way to emphasize to yourself the value of your connection with the spiritual realms.

PATTERNS

You may notice as you become more familiar with the cards that patterns will appear in the layouts. You may have a predominance of one element, or a predominance of stones that apply to a certain chakra or aspect of your life, within any layout. These are strong signals from your guides that give you deeper insights into the meaning of the layouts.

If, for instance, you received all Water element cards in a layout about a relationship with your significant other, this could be an indication that the current situation holds a deep lesson for you that is necessary for your emotional growth. If most of the Water element cards were heart chakra Allies, it would indicate that the lesson involves the ability to feel and express love. If they were throat chakra cards, you would need to focus more on your ability to express your needs, emotions, and personal truth within the relationship.

The patterns that develop in a layout can add a great deal of depth to your reading. They uncover layers of deeper insight and understanding that will enhance the meaning of all of the cards you receive. As you become more familiar with using the cards in the layouts, you will be able to perceive the deeper levels of meaning that the Crystal Allies provide through the use of card patterns.

AFFIRMATIONS

You will notice that at the end of each stone's information there is an affirmation that relates to the energy of that particular mineral. These affirmations are tools that you can use to help yourself change the patterns of the situation or aspect you are working on.

Readings with any divination deck are simply representations of the dominant patterns in your life at this moment. You can change these patterns by finding the lesson behind them and integrating that knowledge into your being. Affirmations are a wonderful tool for doing this because they are an immediate action that you can take to integrate the lesson at hand.

If there is a particular stone or aspect of your reading that speaks to your heart, I would suggest that you begin to practice the corresponding affirmation immediately. This signals to yourself and to your guides that you are ready and willing to change the patterns that have been established in your life.

The use of sound vibration to create resonance with certain frequencies of energy has been a meditative tool for thousands of years. An opera singer's ability to shatter glass with sound is a powerful demonstration of the transformative power of sound vibration on physicality.

When we speak affirmations we are setting up a field of resonance within our own bodies and our environment. This resonant field changes the vibration of everything that comes in contact with it. In this way, we are able to create change in our lives by changing the words that we choose to speak. The use of affirmations can be a powerful way for you to align your life and energy with particular frequencies of vibration.

When you use the affirmations in the Crystal Ally Cards you will find yourself changing your personal vibration, as well as that of your environment. Allow yourself to resonate with the words and the vibration that they create. It is a powerful way to invite the energy of the Crystal Allies into your life!

HEALING WITH
THE CRYSTAL ALLY CARDS ™

As you may have guessed by now, the Crystal Ally Cards™ can be used as more than just divinitory tools. When this concept was originally gifted to me by the Crystal Allies, I saw the potential for the cards being used as vibrational healing tools. Used alone or in conjunction with the actual stones that they represent, they can be valuable tools to use in the diagnosis and treatment of energetic imbalances.

I have already discussed how, with conscious resonance, the cards can be gateways to accessing the energetic vibrations of the Crystal Allies. In this chapter, I will outline some basic practices that you can use to turn the divinitory card layouts into healing grids.

USING STONES
IN CONJUNCTION WITH THE CARDS

The Crystal Ally cards are wonderful tools for the exploration of the energies of gemstones and crystals. As powerful as they are, however, they cannot take the place of the resonant bodies of actual crystals and stones. Even the advanced Crystal Resonance Therapist, who has been trained to experience the energies of crystals and stones through the energetic field of the Earth, still uses crystals and stones for healing purposes. They are, in fact, the most powerful tools we can use to set up fields of resonance within our own aura.

One way in which we can utilize the Crystal Ally Cards to their full potential is by combining them with the stones that they represent. There are some wonderful ways that we can use stones in conjunction with the cards to turn layouts into powerful healing tools. Using stones in conjunction with the cards, you can also practice the exercise of conscious resonance– thereby increasing the efficacy of the Crystal Ally Cards in divination.

STONE LAYOUT GRIDS

Stone layout grids are an effective way to implant the energy of your card reading into your energetic field. You can do this grid without having the corresponding stones, but using it in conjunction with the actual stones greatly enhances it's efficacy.

To start, do any of the card layouts you are drawn to, except the chakra layout (there is a separate meditation coming up for that one!). After you have done the card layout and studied the interpretation, find a space on the floor where you can place the cards in the layout formation with room enough for you to sit in the center.

Place the cards around you in the same positions they held within the layout. Place the corresponding stone upon each of the cards, and take your place in the center of the cards. Beginning with the first card in the layout, pick up it's corresponding stone and hold it in your non-dominant hand.

Begin speaking the affirmation for that card out loud. Focus on the vibration in your body as you speak the words. Imagine your energetic field changing it's vibration until it matches the vibration that the affirmation carries.

Once you have established resonance with the affirmation, focus your attention on the stone that you are holding. Imagine that you can see or feel it's vibration. Now, sense it's vibration filling you. Hold the vibration for as long as you can, then release it and place the stone back on the card.

Repeat the procedure with each stone in the layout.

When you have repeated all of the affirmations and experienced resonance with each of the stones, sit in the center of the grid and focus upon vibrating with all of the stones simultaneously.

This exercise will help you to realign your energetic systems to vibrate in harmony with the stones you have chosen in your layout. At first, you may experience blockages or difficulty in finding resonance with some or all of the stones. Keep at it, and repeat the exercise over the course of a few days, until you feel that you have been able to attain a resonant state with the stones.

You may notice emotions, memories, visions, or other indications that you are "shaking loose" any blockages that may exist. This is a great sign, as it indicates you are truly shifting your energetic vibration!

CHAKRA WORK

The chakra layout is one of the most intense and in-depth layouts that I have included in this book. Through the drawing of cards, you are able to gain insight into the issues that surround each of the chakras in the body. In CRT, we use a 12 chakra system, but for the sake of simplicity and clarity, I have utilized a seven chakra system for the layout.

There are two ways in which you can use the Crystal Ally Cards in conjunction with stones to balance and explore the chakras. The first of these is by using the cards as a diagnostic device in the practice of laying on of stones. The second is to do a resonance exercise similar to the one I have just outlined, but with the important difference that you will actually lay these stones on your body, or the body of the person for whom you are doing the reading.

LAYING ON OF STONES WITH THE CRYSTAL ALLY CARDS

To use the stones as a diagnostic tool, you must first separate the cards into five piles, one for each of the elemental suites. Fan out each pile, and place the card that represents each element next to that element's fan, so that you know which cards to choose from for each chakra.

The Earth element pile is used to draw the first chakra card, the Fire element pile supplies the second and third chakra cards, the Water element pile furnishes the fourth and fifth chakra cards, and the Air element supplies the sixth and seventh chakra cards. You will also pull one card from the Earth element to represent physicality, and one card from the storm element pile to represent spirituality.

Beginning with the first chakra, select a card from the Earth element pile. This is the stone that should be placed upon the first chakra in a body layout. Continue selecting the cards for the chakras from their equivalent element until all of the chakra cards have been drawn. Now you may pull the physicality card from the Earth element pile, and the spirit card from the Storm element pile.

If you are using the cards to diagnose stones to use on yourself, you may now lie down and place the stones over the appropriate chakra. Place the spirit stone in the non-dominant hand, and the physicality stone in the dominant hand. If you are doing this layout for another person, you may place the stones upon their body as you draw the corresponding card.

Now focus or direct your partner to focus upon drawing Light energy into the body with each breath. Sense the energy of the stones filling your body and energy field. Allow any stress or resistance to be released with the exhale, as you draw in energy with your inhalation.

Continue to meditate in this way until you feel you have achieved resonance with the energies of the stones, or until you are guided to stop. Always clear your stones after practicing this exercise, by rinsing in cold water and placing in the sun, or by placing them upon a large clear quartz cluster.

Don't worry if the stones that you choose for this layout aren't exact matches for the chakras. The Crystal Allies will guide you to choose the stones whose resonant field will be most helpful to you. As long as a stone is within your energetic field, you will receive it's benefits. It does not have to be directly over the chakra in order to produce results.

This exercise is great in helping you to experience the effects of strong vibrational fields upon your own energies. By practicing conscious resonance with the stones in this layout, you will feel more clear and balanced, and may experience the clearing of blockages or stagnation in your life.

RESONATING WITH THE CHAKRA LAYOUT

The second way in which you can use the Crystal Ally Cards in clearing and attuning the chakras is through using the chakra card layout. In the chakra card layout, you do not separate the cards into their elemental suites. Instead, you draw the cards intuitively, trusting the allies to guide you to the particular vibration that you need in order to help balance your chakras.

In using this layout, you will often draw stones for a particular chakra that would not normally be associated with that chakra. For instance, you may draw Larimar for the first chakra, even though it is considered to be a fifth chakra stone in the classical practice of laying on of stones.

Since the first chakra is where we process our physical existence, we could interpret the appearance of Larimar in this place as meaning that you may need more nurturance in your life. Perhaps you are giving too much to others, and not receiving the nurturance you need in order to be balanced. By using Larimar on the first chakra, you would be directly treating the need for nurturing energy in that chakra. So do not be concerned if you are guided to place stones in areas where they would not normally be used. The Crystal Allies will guide you to choose those stones that are for your highest benefit.

To begin, do the Chakra spread in the layout chapter, focusing upon asking for those stones that will most help you to come into balance.

Once you have drawn the cards, you may then do a stone layout upon your body with the corresponding stones.

As you place the stones upon you, focus upon drawing light energy up through your feet and out the top of your head. Beginning with the first chakra, repeat the affirmation for the stone you have chosen for that chakra. How does this affirmation make you feel in this chakra? Focus upon drawing light into the chakra through the stone that is upon it. Fill the chakra with the energy of the stone. When you have filled the first chakra, you can then repeat the process with the others.

You can do this exercise with the cards alone as well. Simply meditate upon the card as you draw Light energy into the chakra.

THE DAILY CARD

Another way in which you can use the Crystal Ally Cards™ is by choosing a daily card and stone to meditate upon and carry with you throughout the day. In the practice of conscious resonance, it is useful to choose each day a concept or ideal which the practitioner holds in her mind in order to create resonance in her life with the vibration of the ideal. Gemstones can be extremely useful in reinforcing this practice by setting up a physical vibratory field within the practitioner's aura.

To do this practice, choose a card from the deck each morning . Holding the corresponding stone in your non-dominant hand, read the description of the card, then meditate upon it's keyword and affirmation. Draw the energy of the stone into your body. Feel your energetic system beginning to resonate with the energy of the stone. Focus upon holding this field of resonance as you consciously vibrate with the stone and card.

As you move through your day, carry the stone with you as a reminder of this energy. Each time you think of it, hold the keyword and affirmation of the card in your mind as you draw in the energy of the stone.

This practice is also useful when one wishes to work upon a specific area or issue in one's life. You can either ask a question of the deck and work with the card you are guided to choose, or you can choose a specific card because of it's energetic properties. In either instance, you can use the corresponding stone as a reinforcement tool throughout the day.

USING THE CARDS ALONE

Any of the exercises outlined in this chapter can be done with the cards alone, though it may take some practice before you are able to experience the energies of the stones as strongly through the cards as you would if you were using the stones themselves.

The cards can be used as vibrational tools directly upon the body. When one does not have access to the stone that corresponds to a card, one can focus upon creating resonance with the stone through the energetic field of the Earth, or by simply asking the Crystal Allies to aid you by transferring the vibration to your energy field. It can be surprising how well the use of intent works in connecting with the stone energies in this way!

Experiment with connecting with the energies of the crystals and stones through the use of the cards. Soon, you will be able to notice perceptible differences in the energies you receive from different cards. With practice, you can use these energies as vibrational medicine.

Meditations

CONNECTING WITH Your Crystal Allies

Crystal Allies are the conscious energies of crystals and stones, which you can call upon to aid you in gaining insight into, or affecting change in, your life situations. Crystal Allies are conscious energies, and they do respond to thought. The Ally of one type of stone will be able to communicate different information and understanding from the Ally of another stone. For instance, the Rose Quartz Ally will be of a different vibration, and will give different teachings and lessons, from the Ruby Ally.

Connecting with your Crystal Allies is a simple yet powerful procedure that can greatly enhance the results you get using this deck and your own crystals and stones. This meditation and layout reveals your totem stones, those Allies whose energies you have chosen as the main lessons and forces in your life. To do this meditation, you need to set aside an hour of undisturbed time, as it is necessary to spend time with each of your Crystal Allies to gain the information and understanding it has to give you.

This meditation is most effective when it is used in conjunction with the Crystal Ally layout. I have written the meditation to be done in conjunction with that spread, but you can also use the same basic steps to connect with your own stones, substituting actual crystals for the cards. Become familiar with the meditation by reading it several times before beginning, or have a friend read it to you as you meditate and read the cards.

To begin, find a comfortable position in a quiet room, away from distractions. Spread the cards in a fan shaped arc in front of you, within easy reach. Begin the meditation by breathing deeply several times. This is a signal to your body that you are about to enter a meditative state.

As you inhale, focus on breathing in relaxation and peace. As you exhale- imagine yourself releasing all of the tensions of the day. Continue the process of inhaling peace and exhaling tension for several minutes, or until you feel relaxed and energized.

When you feel as though you have settled your mind enough to begin, close your eyes and sense yourself sitting in a beautiful place in nature. Allow yourself to feel protected and safe, relaxed and at peace. In this place in nature, you are sitting upon the ground with the Earth beneath you. You may be leaning against a tree or a rock, but sense that you are totally supported both beneath you and behind you.

In this place you are surrounded by the beauty and energy of nature. As you sit quietly, begin to sense the energy field of the Earth, either as Light, a sound, or a sensation that surrounds and fills you with it's vibration.

With each inhalation, imagine that you are drawing the Earth's energy into your physical body. Sense it filling you with it's vibration. In your mind, imagine that each cell in your body is changing to match the frequency of the Earth's vibration.

Sense the change in your body as you begin to draw the Earth's energy up through your feet. With each breath the energy moves upward through your body, into your legs, your thighs, hips, and abdomen.

With each inhale, you draw the energy further, until it fills your chest, shoulders and arms. Allow the energy to move up your neck, vibrating away tension, and filling the cells there with energy. Draw the Earth's energy into your head; feel it spilling out the top of your head and running back down the outside of your body and into the Earth.

Continue breathing the energy up and out of your body until you feel that you are vibrating with the frequency of the Earth. Allow your body to come into alignment with the energy of the planet. When you feel that you have 'tuned' into the frequency of the Earth, begin your meditation by offering thanks to the Earth for the gifts received.

When you have given thanks to the Earth and the Divine Creator (or whatever name you choose), open your heart area, and with humility, state your intention of opening to the wisdom of the Crystal Allies. State that you wish to declare your path for the highest good of all concerned, and that you are open to Divine Will as it works through the Allies and all beings in the Universe.

Sense a gathering of consciousness around you. These are the Crystal Allies and other spirit guides who have come to aid you on your path. Greet them and thank them for coming.

When you feel ready, hold your non-dominant hand about one inch above the cards and move it slowly back and forth until a card makes itself known to you through touch or intuition. Draw the card from the deck, and hold it in your hand. Look at the card that you have chosen until you are familiar with it. Then, close your eyes and focus your attention on the card in your hand.

As you sense the card in your hand, ask the Ally energy of the card to come to you through the card. Open your energy and embrace this Ally, allowing it's energy to fill and surround you.

Notice how the energy of this Ally makes you feel. Do you sense the energy more in one part of your body or another? Does the energy of this Ally create any emotions or thoughts for you? Notice any sensations, emotions, or other messages that may come. All of these impressions are gifts to you from your Crystal Allies. They are all valuable messages that may bring insight or understanding into aspects of your life.

Allow yourself to resonate fully with the energy of the Ally that you have chosen. Breathe the energy into your body, allowing it to penetrate into each cell and molecule of your being. Bring yourself in tune with this being that has come to guide you.

When you feel that you have experienced the energy fully, thank the Ally for sharing it's energy with you, and place the card to the side. Repeat the process of choosing and invoking the energies of your Crystal Allies until you have chosen seven Allies.

When you have experienced the energies of these stones, you may then go to the book and look up their messages. The book is only a guideline. The real information is what you have just experienced with your Crystal guides.

The Allies that you receive in this layout are your Totem Allies. These special stones and their energies indicate the primary energies and lessons that you have chosen for this lifetime. These Allies have no particular order. You may wish to carry or wear these stones in a pouch to remind you of their guiding influences, and to aid you in connecting with your gemstone teachers.

Cleansing the Chakras

The Chakras are energetic centers in the body and within the aura that are crucial to the flow of life force energy throughout your being. The balance and health of your chakras can determine the health and balance of your physical, emotional and spiritual levels of existence. When these energetic centers are blocked or unbalanced, the flow of energy through the meridians of the body is disrupted, which can result in poor health, depression, and a general feeling of fatigue.

Crystal Resonance Therapy™ utilizes a twelve chakra system; but because these meditations are meant to be simple and efficient, I am utilizing the classic seven chakra model. Each chakra has a related color ray, the seven together reflecting the colors of the rainbow. When white light is beamed through a prism, it separates into the equivalent of seven colors. This shows us that in order to become Light ourselves, we must embody the energies of all seven rays. This means opening, clearing, and energizing all seven of the physical chakras. The remaining five chakras are non-physical chakras, and therefore are not tied to any particular color ray. They are best worked with through the vibration of white or golden light.

It is best to do this exercise while sitting in an upright position with your back well supported. Take several deep breaths, signaling to your body that you are entering the meditative state.

When you feel relaxed, begin to pretend that you are a seed. For you to grow, you must send roots deep into the Earth. Sense these roots beginning to sprout at your tailbone.

With each breath, imagine them beginning to grow down into the Earth, branching and multiplying as they sink into the dark warm soil. Feel these roots growing further and further down, until you can imagine that your roots have reached the center of the Earth.

When your roots have grown down into the planet, sense them beginning to draw energy back up through the root system and into your physical body.

Mentally give thanks to the Great Earth Mother for the energy you are receiving from her. When the energy has risen into your tailbone, sense the energy taking the form of the color red, and feel it filling your pelvis and legs with warmth and energy.

Notice any sensations you may have, especially emotions or ideas that may be released as you breathe the color red into your pelvis. When you feel as though you have filled that area with the color vibration of Red, sense it beginning to radiate out from your pelvis, filling your energetic field with it's vibration.

Now breathe deeply as you draw the energy from your roots up into your navel area. As the energy moves up from your pelvis, it changes in color from red to orange.

Breathe the energy into your abdominal region until you feel as though you have saturated that area fully with the color orange. Allow the energy to radiate outward each time you exhale, filling your energy field with the vibration of orange. Again, be aware of any information that you may receive from resonating with this vibration.

Now draw the energy upward into your solar plexus area. As the energy moves into your rib cage, it changes to a brilliant yellow vibration. Breathe the color into your solar plexus area, about two inches above your navel. Allow the vibration of the color yellow to fill every cell in the area of your solar plexus.

Sense yourself as the seed drinking in this nourishing vibration. Allow the energy to radiate out from your solar plexus area to fill your energy field. Notice the resonance that this color vibration creates in you. When you feel that you have fully experienced this vibration, draw the energy from your root into your heart area.

As the energy moves into your heart and chest area, it's color changes to a vibrant green ray. Breathe the color vibration into your chest, and sense it filling your arms and hands, radiating from your palms as loving, healing energy.

Allow any resistance to be released, along with any emotions or other experiences that may have been held there. Radiate the color out from your heart to fill your energy field, until it is glowing with the vibration of the color green.

Now draw the energy upward again, sensing it changing from green to a beautiful turquoise or sky blue color. Sense your throat and neck becoming filled with this vibration of blue, as you draw in more energy with each breath.

Allow the vibration to fill your vocal cords, releasing any stagnation of energy there. As your throat and neck fill with the vibration of light blue, be aware of any sounds or experiences stored there that may be signaling for release. When you have fully experienced this vibration, radiate it's energy outward to fill your aura.

Breathe in deeply, drawing more energy upward from your roots and into your head, filling it with a beautiful indigo vibration. Sense a point between and just above your eyebrows. Sense the energy filling the center of your head and radiating outward, sending indigo vibrations throughout your energy field. Allow yourself to experience any images or information that may come to you as you breathe the energy through this area.

When you feel as though your energy is resonating with the Indigo Vibration, draw the energy upward once again until it fills the very top of your head, your crown chakra.

Sense the energy becoming a brilliant violet color, creating a sphere of violet flame just above the top of your head. The violet vibration fills your head, bringing your consciousness upward. Allow yourself to recognize any information, emotions, or experiences that may be released by this color vibration.

When you feel as though you have been saturated with this violet vibration, bring your attention to the very top of your head.

Just above your crown, there is a tiny sprout of light beginning to emerge. Sense the energy being drawn up through your roots, and through each of the your chakras. Sense the energy rising up to feed this shoot of light that is emerging from the top of your head. Sense it growing larger and stronger, reaching up toward the brilliant light of the sun.

As it reaches upward, nourished by the energy that is flowing through your body, it begins to draw in the light of the sun, sending this powerful energy down through your energetic systems. As the Light from the sun enters a chakra, it radiates outward to fill your aura with brilliant Light. Draw the light into each chakra, and down into the root system you have created. Send the light energy back into the Earth with your blessings and thanks.

You are a seed which has sprouted, the roots feeding the plant, and the plant in turn feeding the roots. This double helix energy flow through the body balances and energizes the chakras which you have just consciously opened. When you are ready, you may open your eyes and return to the room.

When you were sensing the color vibrations, were there any that were particularly difficult for you to sense and experience? This can indicate a chakra which may be blocked. If it is difficult for you to sense a color, you may want to have something nearby that is the color you are having difficulty with. During the meditation, you can gaze at this object, giving yourself an exact ray to work with.

You can use this meditation anytime you are feeling as though you need to energize and balance yourself.

Experiencing the Elemental Allies

The world is alive with forces and energies that can be powerful Allies for creating your reality in a joyful and graceful way. These forces are conscious beings, similar to a group mind, that can interact with human consciousness. Indeed, you interact with these forces in the microcosm of your own body each day. You carry the forces of Fire in your energy, Earth in your bones and tissues, Water in blood and fluids, and Wind in your breath and the gasses of your body. Thought and consciousness is akin to Storm, which permeates and effects all.

In our culture, we are prone to attempting to control the natural forces around us, subjugating them for our own exploitation. This attempt to enslave nature is exactly the wrong mindedness that has gotten us into such a mess ecologically, socially and spiritually. These natural resources are as much a part of us as our own mind, and when they are abused we suffer as well.

I urge you to approach these forces with respect and honor. I use the words '"commune" and "prayer" when speaking of these forces because our interaction with them should be from a place of humility and openness. We have much to learn from the voices on the wind and the music of Water, the dance of the fire and the heartbeat of the Earth. Treat these beings as your teachers, not your slaves, and you will be initiated into a wonderful realm of communion with creation.

In practicing this meditation, you will be initiating your experience with the Elemental Allies. This is an introduction of sorts, and is meant to be an opportunity for you to experience the energies of the Allies, while allowing them to become more familiar with your energy patterns as well. In healing practice and deeper meditations, these Allies would be approached separately, and for a specific purpose. I encourage you to experience these energies one at a time in more thorough meditations, once you have gotten the feel for their energies.

To practice this meditation, it is helpful to have ready the elements that you will be invoking. A small dish of dirt or a special stone can represent the Earth element. A small dish of water that you can immerse your hand in, and a small towel, will represent the Water element. A lit candle will represent the force of Fire, and a stick of incense will stand for the force of the Wind. If you are sensitive to smells, you can do this meditation by an open window or utilize your own breath for the Wind element.

Have these elements close at hand, so that you can see and touch them easily from a seated position. Set aside twenty minutes to a half hour for this exercise, making sure that you will not be interrupted. It is best if you do this meditation after you have done the Cleansing the Chakras meditation, as balanced and clear chakras will enhance the experience.

You may wish to pull the elemental cards from the Crystal Ally deck, and place them in front of you so that you can reach them easily. These cards can be used to focus your communication with the Elemental forces, adding to your experience of their energies.

If possible, do this meditation while sitting in the upright position. As in the chakra meditation, you will be drawing energies up through your central chakric column. I have clearly delineated each elemental level of the exercise, so that you can, if you choose, experience only one element in a sitting. If you find yourself drawn to a particular elemental energy, you can do only that portion of the exercise to reinforce the connection.

To begin, take several deep breaths, signaling to your body that you are entering the meditative state. Sense a cord extending down from your feet into the Earth beneath you. This cord extends down into the ground like a root, slowly delving deeper and deeper into the Earth.

EARTH

Take the pot of Earth in your hands, holding it so that it rests in your lap. As you imagine the root extending down from your feet, sense similar roots beginning to emerge from your hands, spreading into the pot of Earth like the roots of a flower.

When you sense your roots firmly established in the planet and the pot of Earth that you hold in your lap, send energy from your heart down through your arms and legs, and out through the root system into the Earth. Send the Earth greetings and Light, imagining your own energy and the energy of your spirit filling your root system. This Light of your spirit is your gift to this Ally, to honor the energy of the Earth.

When you have given your energy to the Earth in greeting, begin a prayer of thanks, offering gratitude for the gifts that the Earth supplies you with each day– from the food that you eat, to the clothes that you wear, the fuel that you burn, and the constant energetic support you receive through the planet's energy field. Give thanks for all that this being does for each and every creature upon the planet.

When you have offered your gratitude, you may call upon the energy of the Earth to make itself known to you . Ask that it share it's energy with you so that you may learn and serve all beings. When you receive a positive response– either as a sense of acknowledgement, a mental message, or a flow of energy, begin to draw the energy of the Earth in through your hands and feet, filling your entire body with the vibration of the Earth Ally.

When you have filled yourself with this energy, and experienced its effects upon your own energetic systems, send the Earth Ally thanks for sharing its energy with you, and resume the energy flow from your heart center into the Earth, consciously ending the interaction with an energy of love and thanks. Put the pot of Earth down, allowing the energies to dissipate.

FIRE

Place the lit candle in front of you, where you can easily reach it. Focus once again upon the energy of the roots that extend downward from your feet; and imagine them going even deeper into the Earth, down through the bedrock of the planet to the molten core that exists at the very center.

Open your eyes slightly, just until you can see the light of the flame. Hold your hands near the flame, until you can feel it's heat and energy, but not so close as to be uncomfortable. Once again, sense roots extending from your hands to the center of the flame.

When you have connected with the energy of the flame and the fire at the center of the Earth, send love energy from your heart center out through your root system to the ally of Fire. Give your thanks for the gifts that Fire gives every day– the warmth of the sun and the heat that keeps you comfortable and allows you to cook your food, the fire of electricity that lights your home, and the fire of passion and creativity the burns within you.

When you have given your energy and your thanks to the energy of the Fire, ask that it allow you to access it's energy so that you can learn and serve all beings. When you receive a positive response, begin to draw it's energy in through your root system, allowing it to enter and fill your abdomen, extending out to fill your body and energy with it's light.

Sense the energy of the Fire and it's ability to burn through any blockage you may have, transforming them into pure energy. Allow this energy to fill and surround you, experiencing it's effects upon your energetic systems and physical body.

When you have fully experienced the energy of Fire, again send the light of your own heart center out through your hands and feet, with gratitude, clearing the energy of Fire from your body, and thanking it for the gift of learning.
Set the candle aside, releasing with it any residual energies of the Fire.

WATER

Move the bowl of water in front of you, to where you can easily immerse your hands in it. Again, draw your attention to the energetic roots that you have extended from your feet. Like the roots of a plant, your own roots will naturally be drawn to the element of Water, so that you can receive nourishment from it's energy. Imagine your roots moving downward into the ground, seeking out the water that is hidden there.

Your roots find an underground spring or river, and sink deeply into it's cool water. Immerse your hands in the bowl of water in front of you. Sense energetic roots extending from your hands into the Water.

When you feel that you have connected with the Water through both your hands and feet, again send energy out from your heart chakra and into the Water, gifting it with your energy. Then begin your prayer of gratitude for the gifts that Water gives us each day– the rain that feeds all plants and growing things, the water that we use to bathe and wash in, the water that we drink, the tears of cleansing and release that we cry, the water in our own bodies that keep us alive. Give thanks for the Water's cleansing and soothing energies. When you have given your prayers of gratitude to Water, ask that it share it's energy with you so that you may learn.

When you receive your response, draw the energy of Water up through the energetic roots of your hands and feet, filling your body with the vibration of Water. Sense the molecules of Water within your own body beginning to vibrate in harmony with the Water element. Allow yourself to resonate with the energy of Water, sensing how it's vibration effects your physical and energetic bodies.

When you have filled yourself with the energy of Water, send heart energy once again out through your energetic roots and into the Water. Thank it for it's gift of knowledge while sending it Light. Set the bowl of water aside, releasing the energy of water as you do so.

WIND

For the element of Wind, you may either light the incense, focus upon your breath, or imagine a breeze blowing around you. For this part of the mediation, you will begin to imagine that there are roots emerging, not only from your hands and feet, but also from the rest of your body, growing outward like a halo of Light strands into the air around you.

Imagine that you are surrounded by a gentle breeze. Sense this breeze as it blows across your face, through your hair, and makes the energetic roots that surround you gently sway.

Send energy from your heart out to the breeze through the energy roots that surround you. Send the Wind your prayers of thanks for all that it gives us– the air we breath, a sense of spirit and power, the changing clouds in the sky, a cooling breeze on a hot day, and the guidance it brings us from the Spirit world. Send the Wind your thanks for it's presence in your life.

When your prayers of gratitude are complete, ask that the spirit of the Wind to make it's self known to you, so that you may learn and serve. When you receive a positive response, begin to draw the energy in through the roots that you have extended, allowing it to fill your physical and energetic bodies. Sense your own energy beginning to resonate with the energy of the Wind, allowing the energy to penetrate to the highest levels of your mind.

When you have fully experienced the energy of Wind, send out energy from your heart center once again to end the energetic link. Again state your gratitude for the lessons experienced and knowledge received as you bid the energy farewell.

When you are done, come back to the present moment and write down your experience of the Elemental forces. The experience of these energies builds over time as your acquaintance and interaction with the Elemental beings or Devas strengthens.

It is a good idea to keep a journal of your experiences, as you may be given information on suitable applications for the energies, or the names of your Elemental guides as you progress with the Work.

Each time you connect with these energies, you are balancing and strengthening those aspects of your own energy that correspond to the Elemental that you contact. This can lead to deep cleansing, healing, and a restructuring of your energetic systems.

Please always remember to honor these energies, as they are a part of you, and any attempt to subjugate them (i.e., weather control, fire starting, etc.) can be greatly damaging to your own energetic systems as well as theirs.

Awakening a Crystal

The process of "awakening" a crystal or stone to your personal energy field can greatly enhance the experience of resonance and communion between a human and mineral. By awakening I do not mean that the stone is unconscious until it comes in contact with a human. Crystals and stones experience their lives through the energies that they conduct. This usually means the energies of the natural forces and other minerals around it. When you awaken a crystal or stone, you are awakening it to the experience of working co-creatively with you. You are allowing it to 'get to know you' before you jump in and start using it.

When a crystal is awakened to your energy field, it has the opportunity to fully experience your energetic frequencies. This process allows the stone to adjust it's own energies in order to join with you in your work more fully. As with any new partner, there is usually a period of adjustment when you begin working with a new stone. Awakening your stone speeds that process, and allows you to begin your work sooner and with better results than you would have done otherwise.

While I call this meditation awakening a crystal, the process works in reverse as well. You are also being awakened to the particular energies of the stone you have chosen. In consciously resonating with the stone, you are able to more fully absorb it's lessons and teachings. This speeds your process along as well! A similar meditation to this one is included on my audio cassette tape *Lightstone Awakenings*. This meditation will be a bit shorter due to the written format.

To begin the meditation, find a comfortable sitting position and hold the stone that you wish to awaken in your non-dominant hand. Take several deep breathes to initiate the meditative state, focusing upon releasing tension and breathing in relaxation.

In your mind, imagine yourself on the edge of a beautiful mountain meadow. The sun is shining overhead, and a gentle breeze is blowing. You are sitting by the side of a small stream, underneath an ancient willow tree. Take a moment to breathe in the fresh air, and allow the sunshine to fall on your face. Feel the warmth of the sun above you and the comforting support of the Earth below you.

When you are ready, bring your attention to the stone that you hold in your hand. Know that within this stone is a being of Light who has come to you in order to aid you with your work in this world.

Before you can begin your work together, the crystal needs to be cleansed and made aware of your presence. In your mind, bend down by the stream and submerge the stone in the cool and cleansing waters. Imagine all unnecessary energies being rinsed away as the energy of the water soothes and refreshes the stone. When you feel that the stone is clear, return to your spot in the sun underneath the willow tree.

Hold the stone in your hand, allowing the warm sunlight to fall upon it– filling it with Light and warmth. Sense the sun filling you as well, surrounding you in a cocoon of golden Light. Sense the warmth of the sun seeping into your body, as you relax more deeply.

Begin to draw the Light of the sun in through your heart, feeling it fill your chest with Light. Feel that Light spill down into your arms and hands, filling them with warmth and energy.

As the energy of the Light fills your hands, send that energy into the stone that you are holding, sensing it sinking deeply into the stone, filling it with the energy of your own heart.

When the light of your heart has filled the stone, the stone will begin to send it's own energy back up your arms, into your heart, filling the cocoon of energy that surrounds you until the energy of the stone resonates throughout your entire body.

Send your greetings to the stone, and thank it for coming to you as a willing partner in your Lightwork. Be attentive to any messages or signals that the stone is sending you. Allow yourself to notice where the energy of the stone resonates most strongly in your own energy field. Continue to resonate with the stone as long as you wish.

During this exercise, you may ask the stone how it should be employed, how it should be cared for, or any other questions about how you can best work together.

DIVINATION LAYOUTS

H EAVEN & EARTH

I have called this spread the Heaven & Earth spread because it represents a modified six-pointed star. The Triangle that points up represents Earth, the physical aspects of reality, and it relates to the the manner in which we create and function on this plane. The second triangle,which points downward, is the triangle of Heaven. This triangle represents the spiritual and mental concerns as they relate to our path here on Earth.

This spread is intended to be used once a cycle to determine which stones would be the most helpful for you in the coming cycle of your life. A cycle can be a year, a menstrual cycle, a moon cycle, a seven year cycle, or any period of time that has meaning for you. The stones that you connect with in this spread are setting the stage for the lessons that are coming up as you begin a new cycle. Each level of the spread is a level of your life and experience, providing a rounded, full view of what to expect during the next cycle of your life.

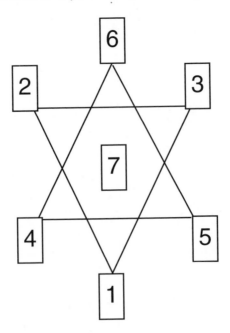

1. This is the Earth star card. This card indicates which life lesson you have chosen to complete in this cycle, or what issue you will be most involved with during the course of the coming cycle. Cards 2 & 3 relate and elaborate on this card and it's lessons for the coming time of growth.

2. This is the Manifest card.This card reveals the manner in which you will be learning the issues of card 1 during the coming cycle. This position can also reveal monetary or abundance issues, and how best to deal with them.

3. This is the Relationship card. This card will indicate the forces in your coming cycle regarding relationships– either business, personal, or friendships– and how they are moving within your life.

4. This is your Creativity card. How are you being guided to express yourself in the coming cycle? What is the force that will aid you best in expressing your creative energy?

5. This is the Communication card. What is the lesson of communication that is developing for you? What is the focus you should be maintaining in your verbal and personal expression to gain the most from the coming cycle?

6. This is the Spirit card. What is the focus of the coming spiritual cycle of growth? How can you best pursue the lessons that are laid out for you in the time to come? Where are your spiritual strengths and weaknesses?

7. This is the Central Sun card. This card indicates the force that will most prominent in your life during the coming cycle, and the one issue around which all others will revolve. This card indicates where you are going to be receiving the most learning , and which issue you need to focus upon the most.

P THE YRAMID

Use this spread to gain a deeper understanding of any issue that may be facing you. Looking down upon a pyramid from the air, it is difficult to see the apex, or termination. The corner stones of the pyramid are easy to see, however, and the symmetry of the beautiful structure becomes even more apparent than from the ground. In life it is often difficult to see the center of a situation. We can easily forget that we are the one point from which all other points in our life emerge.

The apex of an ancient pyramid was the point through which all energy traveled down into the base. Like the pyramid, you are the apex of your creations. Through you, situations become manifest. This spread will aid you in understanding all of the energies you have employed to create your life.

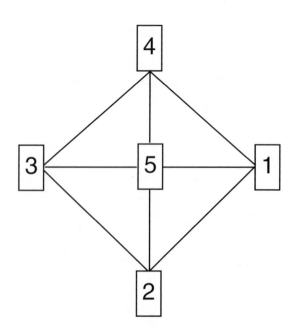

1. This card represents the emotional issue that you are being asked to resolve or explore. Every situation in your life is a lesson created by your Higher Self in order to learn about an aspect of physicality. Emotions are one of the key energies that we employ for creating and exploring our reality on the Earth plane. The Crystal Ally that has appeared here is asking you to explore the emotional issue that it represents, and to relate it to the other cards in the spread to create a complete picture of the lesson involved in the current situation.

2. The second card in this spread represents the physical aspect of the lesson. This aspect relates to physical action, strength, and awareness. Your body is the vehicle through which you create and explore the physical realm. The Crystal Ally that appears here has come to aid you in taking positive action toward the resolution and integration of the current lesson or situation. The old saying, "the Divine helps those who help themselves", is not meant to be a justification of greed or selfishness, but a call for action. Often, the Divine can work through our actions to create magnificent results, if only we will take the initial step, and move forward toward our dreams.

3. The third card in the Pyramid is the card of challenge. What is the obstacle or challenge you have chosen to experience before understanding is reached? Each situation has a light and a dark aspect, an aspect of illumination and one of mystery. This card points toward the unseen influences at work and asks you to consider and understand them so that you can meet them with clarity of mind and purpose.

4. The fourth card is the Spirit card. This card brings a message from the spiritual self, giving guidance and providing support. This card will give you a clearer idea of the spiritual lesson that may be involved in the current situation. The Ally that appears here is a messenger from the Wind Element. Listen carefully to it's direction and open your mind to the answers that are being given to your questions.

5. This is the Self card. At the apex and in the center is the creator, and that creator is you! Remember that you can create your reality into anything you wish, if you remain centered and open to Spirit. The self card indicates what quality or lesson is the driving force behind the creation of the situation. This would be the base emotion or vibration for the entire experience. In resonating fully with the energy of the Ally that appears here, you will consciously initiate the acceleration of the lesson to it's perfect end.

THE

CHAKRA SPREAD

This spread will aid you in identifying those energetic areas in your life that may need special attention. It can also be used to find stones which could be used effectively in treating an affected area of your experience. For this spread, we will use the classical East Indian chakric model that is based upon the seven major chakras in the body. Each chakra in this model rules over a particular issue in one's life, as well as a particular area and function of the body.

To do this spread, shuffle the cards thoroughly, allowing some to become reversed in position. Spread the cards face down in a fan in front of you, so each card has an edge showing. Allow your mind to become calm and, holding your non-dominant hand about two inches above the deck, allow it to "scan" back and forth over the cards until you touch a card. Drawing that card out of the deck, place it in the first position, and continue the process until all seven cards are pulled. You may lay out the cards from left to right, as long as you keep track of which card corresponds to each chakra.

|7| Crown
|6| Third eye

|5| Throat
|4| Heart

|3| Solar Plexus
|2| Naval

|1| Root

1. The card in the first position is the physical experience card. The base chakra is located at the base of the spine near the tailbone. The color of this chakra is red. The base chakra is responsible for the basic needs of existence. The physical vitality of a person can be affected by this chakra, as can one's basic opinions and beliefs about the nature of life and how to live. This is the chakra through which we process and 'ground' our experiences, and through which we eliminate any unnecessary or unwanted energies.

This chakra rules over the lower intestines. It is involved in a person's practicality and ability to manage the daily aspects of life— food, clothing, work, etc. The card that appears in this position is providing insight into how you process your life and what you need to focus on in order to experience life to the fullest.

2. The second card is the creativity card. The navel chakra is located about two inches below the navel, and it rules over passion, creativity, and the ability to manifest your dreams and ideas. It is related to the reproductive organs and the sex drive. The color of this chakra is orange.

The card in this position gives insight into the manner in which you are creating your experiences. The ability to manifest your dreams on the Earth plane is an important part of living effectively. This card will give you a deeper understanding of what you need to focus on to allow your dreams to manifest into reality.

3. The third card is the will card. The will is located in the Solar Plexus chakra, about two inches above your navel. The Solar Plexus chakra is the point of attachment for the emotional body. It is in the will center that your drive for experience rests. The will is a very important aspect of creation. How the will is used determines the karma associated with your creations.

How do you present yourself to others? How do you relate to others emotionally and energetically? Are you presenting yourself one way and living another? It is through this chakra that you learn to "walk your talk", and utilize the Will to bring the body in line with the spirit and the mind.

The card that is in this position is showing you the way to "right relations" with yourself and others. Through understanding the properties of the stone that has chosen to appear here, you can gain a better understanding of how you interact with others, how you can best use your will to create change on this plane, and how others may be seeing you.

4. The fourth card in this spread is the heart card. The heart chakra is located between the nipples in the center of the chest. This chakra is the first of the higher chakras. The higher chakras are less concerned with the workings of the world and more concerned with the spiritual aspects of life. The heart chakra governs the physical heart as well as the ability of an individual to give and receive love. This chakra is also concerned with regulating the amount of love and beauty that one feels for one's creations, otherwise known as self-esteem. Without love of the self, there can be no true love for others.

The card in this position is reminding us of how we can best experience and express love and appreciation for all of the gifts of the universe. What are your strengths? What do you need to pay attention to and improve? The stone in this position will guide you to feeling more love for yourself and others.

5. "What I speak, I create" is the message of the fifth position. The throat chakra is located in the hollow between the collar bones, and governs our spoken expressions. The words that we speak every day determine what we perceive to be the truth of our lives. If we consistently speak negatively, we will perceive our lives to be the negative that we have spoken of. If we constantly say "I don't have enough", or "I never get anything good", then we will experience ourselves as being poor and unlucky. We must always be aware of the power of our spoken words.

The card in the fifth position is reminding us that what we speak becomes manifest. What do we need to affirm to create an abundant, loving, happy life? What have we been affirming that is creating our present life? The stone ally that has chosen this position to appear in will guide you to affirm only what is in the highest good for all concerned.

6. The card in this position is the "far sight" card. The third eye has traditionally been the chakra associated with psychic ability and powers. It is located between and slightly above the eyebrows. This energetic center affirms, "What I believe to be true, I see reflected around me". What we perceive in the world is really only a reflection of our beliefs. Once we alter our beliefs, we will see a new reality unfold.

The card in this position is pointing out the beliefs that we need to reevaluate or reinforce in order to fulfill our mission on the Earth plane. What is it that we need to see in order to understand our next step? Look before you leap!

7. This final card is the I AM card. The crown chakra is located at the top of the head, and is our "spiritual bellybutton". It is through this chakra that we can gain connection to higher levels of being, and commune with the energetic beings that are all around us. This is the chakra that appears as a halo of light in spiritual art. This is the doorway to the higher realms.

The stone Ally that has appeared in this position is bringing direct communication from your highest guides. It is an indicator of what you need to focus upon to attain the next step on your spiritual path.

THE
ELEMENTAL ALLY SPREAD

The natural Elements of the Great Mother Earth are powerful Allies to have in invoking change and in your life. In this spread, you investigate the role that each Elemental force is playing in your current life situation. Each position is ruled by a direction, and the Elemental force that is associated with that direction. The Crystal Ally that appears in a given position adds deeper levels of understanding of where your life situation is leading.

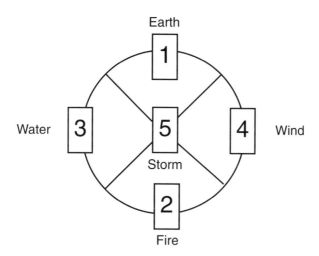

1. Earth– Foundations

The Earth position is the place of beginnings and foundations. This aspect can reveal to you the key issue that supports all of your creations at this time. What is the lesson for the phase of growth you are experiencing now? In understanding the force that is the underpinning for all of your experiences, you will be able to foresee the effects of actions as they are taken.

The Earth element is the bones of your next phase of growth. When you invoke the power of the Ally which has appeared here, you are invoking the energy that is the very basis of the experiences your current path is leading you toward.

2. Fire – Transformation

The second card is in the house of action. It is through action that we create our reality and our experience. It is often difficult to find the correct path of action in any situation. The Ally that has appeared here is gifting you with knowledge of a course of action that will aid you in moving through this current cycle of growth. The energy invoked here is always an energy of transformation. You are constantly growing and changing, transforming yourself into a new and more knowledgeable person. By employing the energy that has appeared to you here, you will be able to make the transformation that is necessary to learn the lessons of the current phase of your life.

3. Water– Introspection

The third Elemental force, that of Water, is in the West. This is the direction and the Element for introspection. Water represents the emotions, motives, and inner energies that are dominant at this time. Through introspection, the study of one's own self, we gain much knowledge of why we create the experiences we do. The insight that Water energy provides is that of seeing below the surface. If there are any unseen or unconsidered forces at work in the present cycle of learning, Water will reveal them through the Crystal Ally that appears here.

Water also represents the force of cleansing. Cleansing is a crucial step to growth, because it allows old energies and experiences to be released, making way for the new, and assuring that outmoded desires, thought forms, and beliefs aren't currently effecting the creations you wish to manifest.

Call upon the energy of Water to aid you in clearing these aspects from your life, and invoke the Crystal Ally that has appeared in Water's home. This Ally will point out to you the area that needs attention and cleansing the most.

4. Wind– Spirit Voices

The East is the place of Wind. Wind is the voice of Spirit. On the Wind you can receive guidance from your highest guides and angels. The Crystal Ally that appears in the place of the Wind is bringing you a message from your guides and Higher Self. This Ally also offers you a path you can use in communicating with the Spirit realm.

The power of Wind is a bridge between the physical and the spiritual realms. It's energy lives in your breath, is carried in your blood, and moves around and through you constantly. When you resonate with the Crystal Ally that has appeared here, you are creating a connection with Spirit. By opening to this realm, you are opening to the first levels of remembrance of who and what you truly are.

5. Storm– Wholeness

Storm is the point of both creation and destruction. It is the moment that exists between the worlds. When all of the other Elemental Allies join together in a moment of wholeness and power, the element of Storm is manifested. Storm combines the powers of clarity, cleansing, transformation and physicality. The Crystal Ally that appears in the house of Storm represents the outcome of the situation if all other elements are honored.

The Storm Ally card represents you at this moment. It is the card that connects the other Elements into a unified whole. Whatever Ally appears here is the prophet that has come to tell you of your mission at this time. By employing the energy or frequency it represents, you are becoming the center point of your own wheel of creation, around which the other aspects revolve.

THE

T RINITY SPREAD

The Trinity spread is a simple and direct spread that gives you an overview of the situation at hand. The Trinity spread is based on the three levels of being– Body, Mind, and Spirit. Each of these aspects plays a part in each experience we create for ourselves. This spread gives each of these aspects a voice with which to guide you.

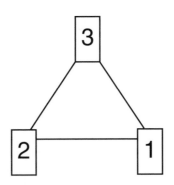

1. This card represents the physical aspect, and indicates the action called for in the current situation. Every one of our actions is an expression of thought on some level. The Ally that has appeared in this position is indicating the idea that will guide your actions in the appropriate direction for the highest good of all concerned.

Consider the actions that have led you to this point, and the choice of actions that you have before you. Now hold the key word for this Ally in your mind as you review them. Your Crystal Ally will give you clear direction as to which action is most appropriate to take at this time.

2. The card in this position represents the Mind aspect– that of thought and conscious creation. The Ally appearing in this position is revealing the key lesson behind the situation. It can also indicate the thoughts which will be most productive for you and which would aid you in creating the most positive experience of the situation.

3. This is the Spirit card. The Ally in this position is bringing direction and guidance from the Higher Self and other guides to help you in understanding the energies behind the creation. This card represents the highest vibration available to you now. When called upon, this vibration will aid you in overcoming obstacles that may challenge you along the way. This is the "guardian Angel" card, and it is a powerful Ally to aid you on your path.

Earth Element Allies

EARTH

Earth

On this card the mountain slumbers beneath a cloak of snow, indicating a time of rest and recuperation after a long season of hard work. The element of Earth occupies the place of the North on the great wheel, representing a time of retreat deep within the inner world in order to regain one's strength for the coming season of growth and activity.

On the mountain there is an entrance to a sacred cave. In the practice of traditional shamanism the cave is the gateway to the underworld, a magical place where spirit helpers await the shaman to aid her in her healing and magical work. This cave symbolizes the womb of nature. It is through a cave that humanity is born into the world, and it is deep within a cave that we are laid to rest, until we take a new body and emerge once again from the womb of the Great Earth Mother.

The elemental force of Earth is the manifestation of the energy of life. The strength of this element can mold matter from energy, forming the very basis of physicality. The Earth represents the bones of the Great Earth Mother, upon which all nature is constructed. Without the immense and pervasive energy of the Earth element, there would be no cohesiveness to the energy of nature; there would be no life.

This natural force is the spectrum of Light energy that provides us with our life force, our physical stamina and energy. The elemental force of Earth relates to the issues of survival, physicality, and the ability to ground and eliminate excess or unwanted energies. It is through this element that we learn to connect and communicate with the other beings that share our world. This element is the densest manifestation of Light energy accessible to us. When we connect with this element, we come to understand the lessons of becoming Light manifested in matter.

Earth is the basis upon which all of creation is built. It is through her fertility and bounty that the great web of life is spun.

This Elemental force is the doorway through which all of our own manifestations are born. It is her frequencies and influence that transform energy into matter and lend form to all ideas and endeavors you choose to focus upon.

The Earth's energy field is influenced powerfully by the two heavenly bodies that dance with her through the heavens. The energy of the Sun, the male aspect, gives light to the Earth Mother so that she may provide for her children. The Moon, or female aspect, sings the song of cycles and fertility, of mystery and introspection. The Earth is in the center, her energy moving first with the sun, then with the moon, creating a great balance of Light and dark, male and female.

These heavenly bodies affect us as well, through the element of Earth. We are constantly immersed in a sea of Earth's vibrations, and through her energy we learn of the dance of life and the law of cycles, and so come to know our own patterns through hers.

It is through the Earth Star chakra, six inches below the soles of the feet, and the root chakra, located at the base of the spine and the pubis, that we are most resonant with this element. When these energetic centers are vibrating in harmony with Earth energy, one is able to function effectively in the physical world and maintain one's basic needs. This promotes a sense of abundance and a willingness to become like the Earth by grounding Light into the physical world. When we are not resonating with Earth energies we can feel spacey, flighty, confused, impotent, and unable to function properly in our lives. A person who is not resonating fully with Earth energy may be scarcity-minded and overly fearful of lack or loss.

When you connect with the immense energy of this Elemental force, you can channel and apply it's frequencies to create form from energy through your own manifestation process. Survival depends upon the ability to manifest your needs into the physical world. In opening to the bounty of the Earth's energy, you are opening to the energy of abundance and prosperity. The Divine Creator placed us here upon this planet because it could support our every need. But we have turned away from the horn of plenty that was set before us, and we have in turn become a people who believe that they never have enough.

In our quest for more we have begun to destroy the very instrument that was created to supply us with all we could ever need. We have not only begun to destroy our own means of survival, but the means of survival for all of the beings that depend upon this planet– plant, animal, and human. It is time to reopen the channels of abundance from the Universe to it's children. To do this we must reconnect with the Earth's energy and in so doing, reconnect to the bounty, strength, and vitality that the Divine Creator has promised all of it's children.

THE MESSAGE

It is through connection to the Earth that we receive an abundance of material prosperity, energy, strength, and support. This Elemental Ally has come to you today to let you know that all of the resources you need are available to you now for the asking. Draw upon the immense store of energy within the Earth, giving back your gratitude and conscious blessing of Light.

Sink your energetic roots into the ground, and allow the planet to replenish your depleted stores. You are being guided to take action and create your reality from the energy you are being offered. Now is the time to undertake the tasks that you may have been putting off as too daunting or impossible. All that you need will be given you by the bounty of the Earth element.

FEMALE POWER

CUPRITE

Cuprite

FEMALE POWER

The Cuprite card places you deep within the Earth, at an ancient altar dedicated to the power of the female aspect of physicality. The cave itself represents the womb of the Earth, from which all physicality springs, and the womb of the female being. The womb is the place of creativity, representing the potent void. This void is the place from which all is created, predating even the Divine Creator. It is the place of potential and the place to which all will return to be born again.

The cave itself is formed from Cuprite, the stone of female power. Cuprite, also called copper pyrite, is the female aspect of the Earth connection triad (Hematite, Pyrite and Cuprite). It forms in apparently opaque, gray, metallic crystals and massive forms. Cuprite has a secret, however. When held to a bright light, Cuprite reveals it's true energies with it's translucent blood red color. Red is a color of power, as it is the color of the life force that is blood. The metallic gray/black color of the stone, when it is not in bright light, reflects the mystery of the void, the potential of the universe. The fact that both of these frequencies are carried by Cuprite reveals its power as an ally of the female aspect of our nature. Red is also the color of the first chakra, encouraging the cleansing, activation and balancing of this vital energy center.

The practice of going within and entering the void from which all creation springs is one of the most ancient and powerful rites of the shaman. The retreat within oneself to consider, meditate, pray and seek Spirit, is an ancient female practice during her moon time. The frequency of Cuprite resonates with the Earth and the Moon within, stimulating our regenerative and healing capabilities. It is the frequency of death and renewal, aiding our physical bodies in reconnecting to the primal life force of the first chakra. It's energy represents the quest for the Great Mystery.

Cuprite is the balancing energy to Pyrite. While Pyrite represents the action of manifestation, which is the male aspect of the Earth connection triad, Cuprite represents the void from which all creation springs. It is this vibration that can lend you the energy and the courage to give birth to your dreams.

THE MESSAGE

Cuprite's appearance in your cards is signaling you to invoke the power of the female aspect of your nature. The answers that you seek lie within your own deepest self. Make the time to find them by moving inward through meditation and solitude. Open yourself to the mysteries of the universe, and to the void where all potential exists.

The appearance of this ally is signaling a "moon time", a time of retreat and seclusion, from which you will gain the insight and strength you need to move forward on your journey. It is time to trust the unseen forces that are at work in your life. Open yourself to the realm of spirit. By moving within, you encourage your inner self to speak and to share with you the secrets of your hidden path.

CHAKRAS: Earthstar and Root chakra
AFFIRMATION: I am the source of creation.

MALE POWER

PYRITE

Pyrite

MALE POWER

In this image, Pyrite hangs in the sky, reflecting golden light and manifesting the energy of the solar male aspect of the Earth element. In order to create life or to function in life, one must have a balance of male and female energy. The male aspect of the Earth element is that which enables us to take action upon the inspiration and ideas we receive when we go within. It is the aspect which gives direction and focus to the creativity of the Universe.

The Sun and the Earth are intimately connected. Without the dynamic energy of the Sun, the Earth would be barren of life. The Earth responds to the proximity and energy of the Sun through the changing of the seasons and the creation of new life. Pyrite represents that solar energy within the Earth itself.

Iron Pyrite is a beautiful golden mineral that is also known as "fools gold". It is the male aspect of the Earth connection triad (Pyrite, Cuprite and Hematite). Pyrite encourages the flow of Earth energy into the body, increasing physical stamina and facilitating it's expression through action. Pyrite brings the Golden ray of mental acuity and learning into the physical body, encouraging action guided by higher knowledge. This Ally aids in the processes of manifestation and creation on all levels.

The male aspect of the Earth is that which supplies the drives that we experience as human animals. It is the energy of the Sun upon the earth, encouraging growth and movement, and it is the Lightening from the sky, the force that drives us to act upon our desires. The Earth Mother has both a male and a female aspect, which are fully balanced and integrated. Each of us also has a male and a female aspect.

Our lives on Earth are spent seeking the balance to our energies, so that we can return to the state of wholeness that we knew before incarnating into the dualistic realm of physicality. When we achieve this balance, we are both male and female in one person, and our skills and talents will allow us to both nurture and provide for ourselves and our community.

When we are young, we embody both aspects of duality within our bodies. We are neither truly male nor female. When we become pre-adolescent, however, our energies begin to polarize. Much of our adult life is spent seeking the balance to the polarity that we have become. Some believe we can find it through a mate or other person who would act as our balancing polarity. In truth, every outward manifestation of the energy that we seek is only a reflection of our inward quest to reunite the male and the female within our own self.

Our ancient elders were honored for their achievement of this balance and the wisdom it brought. The ancient grandfather is able to share with the younger males of the tribe the knowledge that he has gained through a lifetime of seeking his female aspect. This learning would include the value of going within to gain knowledge and guidance, cultivating the ability to nurture, and the power of the mystery within the void.

The ancient grandmother shares with the young women the knowledge and understanding she has gained through her quest of the male aspect. She may teach the necessity of taking action to fulfill one's needs, utilizing one's energy for protection and provision, and the use of the will in the process of creation.

The quest for the alternate side of one's nature is one of the most important lessons we learn in physicality. It brings the knowledge that the polarities of light and dark, male and female, are all simply aspects of a greater whole. Whichever of these polarities we may adopt as a moment's identity, we exist always at our center as the unified whole.

THE MESSAGE

When Pyrite appears in your cards, you are being asked to seek out and employ the male aspect of your self to resolve the current situation. This male aspect is the solar energy that resides within you, encouraging you to take the action that is indicated by your highest guidance. Pyrite speaks of movement, and a time of making yourself into the light of the Sun.

The ability to plant new seeds and to act upon your intuition are nurtured by Pyrite. This Ally is calling you to begin to apply on the Earth plane what you have learned by going within. It is time to manifest the creations that you have conceived, by taking action and expressing your inner truth.

CHAKRA: Earthstar and Root

AFFIRMATION: I plant seeds of light on Earth.

H EMATITE

MANIFEST LIGHT

In this card, Hematite gathers the light from the Universe, and manifests it upon the Earth plane. This represents "Manifest Light, the highest ideal of humanity as we move into the age of light. Hematite has the ability to draw light energy into the most dense most difficult energies. It's red aura indicates it's ability to draw light into the first chakra, manifesting the light body in the human form.

Hematite is a metallic, silver-gray stone that leaves a red streak when drawn across a scratch plate. Because of this red streak, the ancient Greeks felt that Hematite was the solidified blood of the Earth, and so called it "haimatites" or "bloodlike stone". Hematite is the cardinal stone of the Earth Connection triad (Hematite, Pyrite and Cuprite). It represents within that triad the spiritual light behind all creation, and the unity that underlies all duality.

Hematite resonates with the energy of Manifest Light as matter. As an Ally, it aids in drawing the higher frequencies of spiritual energy onto the Earth plane, and grounding that energy into the physical body and physical matter.

Hematite works as an energy regulator, drawing upon and balancing energy where it is needed. If there is a lack of energy, its frequencies aid one in connecting with the Earth Mother and replenishing depleted stores. If there is an overabundance of energy, it will aid in the grounding of that excess energy into the Earth, so that she may use it elsewhere. Hematite strengthens the energetic cord that binds us to the planet, and allows higher frequency energies to enter and flow through the body.

We know that all matter is actually energy that vibrates within a certain range of frequencies. We have come into physicality in order to experience resonance with those frequencies of energy so that we may learn from them. Part of the experiment of physicality is to manifest spiritual Light into the slower frequencies of physicality. This is the process and the goal of our spiritual growth– to bring the vibration of matter into resonance with the vibration of Spirit. To do this, we can consciously connect with the high frequency energy of the Universe, and use our bodies and minds as channels for that energy to be transmitted into the physical realm.

Hematite is the ally that is best suited to aiding us in this important work. By resonating with the energy of Hematite, we become more able to express our highest purpose here on Earth. Through Hematite's guidance and ministration, we are reminded that we are the doorway through which the Age of Light will enter the physical plane.

THE MESSAGE

Hematite has appeared in your cards today to remind you that part of your purpose here on Earth is to bring the Light of Spirit into the physical world through your creations, actions and words. All of the physical realm is composed of varying frequencies of Light. By focusing upon becoming a channel for that Light, you will begin to manifest it into the physical world through your creations and experiences.

Take time throughout the day to focus on expressing the light of Spirit through whatever you are doing. Connect with the Earth element and bring the Light not only into your own body, but onto the planet as well. It is through this expression of Spirit that the Age of Light will be born into the world.

CHAKRA: Earth Star and Root chakra
AFFIRMATION: I am a channel for the Light
on the Earth Plane.

PURIFICATION

BLACK
TOURMALINE

Black Tourmaline

PURIFICATION

In this card, Black Tourmaline creates a vortex of energy, which draws in and purifies other energies with which it comes into contact. Black Tourmaline, or schorl, occurs in massive form and in the form of crystals, usually exhibiting a striated structure. It is the Ally of purification because of it's ability to absorb "negative" or non-usable energy, and to transmute that energy into neutral, usable frequencies. This process of purification clears the energy of any prior intent, allowing it to be redirected in more productive ways. Black Tourmaline is often used in healing environments because of it's ability to absorb released energies and purify them.

Purification has always been acknowledged as a necessary part of spiritual practice. The ritual of purification allows time for the redirection of the mind from daily matters to more spiritual planes. Purification also clears the energy systems of any thoughts or psychic debris that could cause blockages or imbalance if allowed to remain. It is a process of "energetic housecleaning" that is vitally important to anyone who strives for connection to their spiritual path.

One of the most effective ways to purify one's energy is to connect with the Earth. The Earth is the ultimate energetic purifier. She is able to absorb and transmute energies through her core of fire, turning them into clear energetic frequencies that she then emits through her own energy field. Humans have recreated this purification ritual throughout the centuries through the use of the sweat lodge or sauna. This is an ancient practice used by Native Americans and Native Europeans in order to purify their energy before or during prayer.

By pouring water over heated rocks (Earth and Fire elements) to form steam (Water and Wind elements), you are invoking the energies of all of the elemental forces to aid you in purification. While this is a powerful cleansing ritual, it is not readily available to most people in our culture. We do have a more "watered down" version of this purification ceremony, however, that most people partake of on an almost daily basis. This is the ceremony of bathing. Through the use of hot water, we can partake of a similar, though less potent, form of purification.

One can also purify through meditation, smudging with incense or smoke, fasting and prayer, or any ritual that focuses your intention upon cleansing. Once we have received purification, we are able to connect more deeply with our spiritual self, without physical or energetic distractions.

Black Tourmaline's energy invokes the process of purification whenever it is called upon. When you resonate with Black Tourmaline, any superfluous or non-usable energy will be absorbed and purified, then given to the Earth for her use. You will be left cleansed and renewed, and more able to focus yourself upon the task at hand.

THE MESSAGE

When Black Tourmaline appears in your cards, it is encouraging you to undertake a ritual of purification. Perhaps you are holding onto old patterns that no longer serve you. Or maybe you have been exposed to energies that are preventing you from being centered and focused. It is time now to take a spiritual bath, to cleanse your aura and regain a sense of your center and your personal energy.

Call upon the energies of Black Tourmaline. Allow yourself to sense this Ally with you as you transmute any density within your aura or environment into pure, clean, high energy that is available for you to use once again.

If you are experiencing difficulty in connecting with your guidance, try a ritual of purification before you meditate. Take a bath or shower as you focus upon the water cleansing your energy. Take a ritual sweat in a sauna or sweat lodge, or smudge yourself and the room with burning herbs or incense. When you purify your self and release any obsolete thoughts, beliefs, worries, or resentments, you are making room in your life for spiritual gifts to be received.

CHAKRA: Root
AFFIRMATION: My energy is free
from outside influences.
I am centered and clear.

O BSIDIAN

PROTECTION

In this image, Obsidian is nestled in a protective spot above a field of lava. This image represents protection in the face of difficulty or danger. The lava also represents the strong combination of Earth and Fire energies that Obsidian carries.

Obsidian is a natural volcanic glass that is usually black or brown, and can have gray or white ash inclusions. Obsidian has been used for thousands of years in the making of tools and weapons. It is sharp, easily worked, and fairly strong. Because of our ancestral association with Obsidian as a material for weapons and tools, it has been considered since ancient times to be a stone of protection.

Though we no longer use Obsidian for spears and blades, it's role as a protective tool is still valuable. Our ancient ancestors used it as a talisman to turn aside misfortune and bad luck. We can also use it to turn away energies that we do not wish to experience.

This Ally's frequency helps to seal the aura, preventing stray energies from affecting you. This is particularly helpful if you live in a city, where the energy of thousands of people can create an unhealthy amount of energetic "noise". If you find yourself in a situation where conflict is arising, Obsidian's frequencies create a protective shield, preventing you from being sucked into another's power game.

Obsidian is able to "cut" etheric cords that can bind one person to another, preventing others from energetically attaching themselves to your aura and draining your energy.

Obsidian's protective powers are also helpful in dispelling fears and absorbing negative thoughts, so that they do not become manifest. Like Black Tourmaline, Obsidian is able to absorb energy and cleanse it. But instead of transmuting the energy directly, Obsidian uses the energies to create lessons and opportunities for growth for the source of the energy. While protecting it's human partner from the negative impact of the energies, Obsidian will seek to teach the person where the fears and negativity may lie, so that the source of the energy can be cleared.

Obsidian's frequencies are receptive in nature. It's energies are defensive rather than offensive, offering you the opportunity to gain insight through response to the situations around you. Obsidian speaks of the shadows, the unseen, and the mystery. It is a strong psychic stone, initiating inner sight. It will lead you to what is most necessary for you to learn, but not necessarily what is easiest or most pleasant. Because it is a stone of the void, it is unpredictable. In honoring Obsidian's great protective and cleansing powers, you are sure to gain valuable knowledge about your deepest self.

THE MESSAGE

Powerful protection and aid are at your side when Obsidian appears as your Ally. This Ally has come to tell you that you are receiving protection in the situation at hand. Just as the ancients utilized Obsidian as their protecting force when faced with danger or necessity, you may utilize it's power to cut through any difficulties or obstacles that stand in your way.

Obsidian is the power of the receptive. It's greatest strength is in absorbing the energy of others and turning it to it's own use. Stand back and be receptive to what is happening around you. Obsidian will guide you toward the proper action when the opportunity you have been waiting for arises.

CHAKRA: Root

AFFIRMATION: I am protected and provided for by the receptive power of the universe.

LIFE FORCE

RUBY

Ruby

LIFE FORCE

In this image, the receptive human spirit receives life force energy from the Ruby stone. The dark spirit figure represents the void being filled with energy. This energy is the etheric bridge between the potent void and the Light.

Ruby is a corundum that forms in hexagonal, cylindrically shaped crystals, ranging in color from pale pink to deep blood red. Ruby is one of the fabled precious stones of history. In biblical traditions, it has long been thought that Ruby was one of the power stones in the High Priest Aaron's magical breastplate. In the Lord of the Ring trilogy by J.R.R Tolkein, it appears as the stone of adamant in the ring Narya. This was the ring worn by Gandalf the wizard, and was one of the three rings of power that remained unblemished by the Dark Lord's evil.

For centuries, Rubies have been valued for their magical applications, and as symbols of love and virility. The true power of Ruby lies in it's ability to stimulate life force energies. It initiates the Kundalini, or sacred force, which resides at the base of the spine within the first chakra. It's energy opens and clears the first chakra, stimulating the flow of energy from the Earth up the chakric column.

When properly initiated and harnessed, these powerful forces can be used in the manifestation of Spiritual Light, the creation of matter, and in the healing of the physical, mental, and spiritual self. It is a stone that bridges the elements of Earth and Fire, vibrating with the grounding properties of the Earth and the transformative properties of Fire. It has long been prized by magicians and wizards, who use the life force energies to work magic.

Often when we feel run down or overtired, we have developed a block in our energy systems that does not allow the life force energy to rise in our bodies. This creates the feeling of being drained, disassociated, or depressed. Calling upon Ruby as an Ally to aid in the raising of the life force allows you open and clear your blockages, replenish your energy, and reconnect with the life force in all things.

When one is balanced, Ruby can be called upon to initiate the rise of the sacred Kundalini serpent up the spine. The rising of the Kundalini is a powerful spiritual experience that clears the chakras and intiates communion with the sacred Light.

Ruby has the capacity to stimulate sexual desire and energy, or to raise the vibration of excess sexual energy, harnessing it so that one can use it for spiritual ends.

THE MESSAGE

The appearance of Ruby as your Ally signals a time of renewed energy in your life. Ruby speaks of the need to experience the first chakra's primal and potent energy. Practice breathing in through the base of your spine, drawing a cord of energy up through your body and out the crown of your head. Connect with the elements of Earth and Fire, encouraging their energies to rise through you and transform any blockages you may be holding.

The appearance of Ruby can also signal a time of reconnecting with the forces of ritual and magic. When the energies of your first chakra are open and flowing, your store of usable energy is vast. By channeling this energy into current situations or projects, you can create magical transformations in your life. Be aware of how you are applying this energy, however. Using it to manipulate or attach to others will backfire. Draw your energy upward and extend it outward from your higher chakras, so that it can be directed by the higher mind.

CHAKRA: First

AFFIRMATION: I allow the Life force within me
to rise and strengthen my body and mind.

COURAGE

BLOODSTONE

ᛒLOODSTONE

COURAGE

In this image a female warrior braves the crossing of a dangerous and potentially fatal chasm. Not only is she in a precarious position upon the brink of total transformation, but she is also trapped between two high rock faces. She cannot see the other side of the rock toward which she is moving, yet she continues, knowing that she must undertake this act of bravery, even though the reward is not easily seen. In her hand, she carries the shield of Bloodstone to protect her.

Bloodstone is a legendary stone which has been held in high regard by many ancient cultures. Ancient Christians believed that it was formed when the Christ's blood fell from his body on the cross, spotting the green earth with its stain. Because of its bloodlike appearance, it was believed to have powers over wounds and illness, healing both the body and the soul.

Bloodstone's energy combines the green ray of the heart with the red energy of the first chakra. This combination of energies strengthens one's ability to maintain emotional balance when faced with survival issues. It lends courage, or 'heart', when one is confronted with difficult situations. Bloodstone lends strength of mind, firmness of purpose, and confidence when a situation calls for you to take action.

Blood, which is the carrier of life force throughout the body, is pumped by the heart, which is the seat of the emotions.

Bloodstone strengthens and cleanses the blood, increasing the flow of life force to the tissues of the body. It also lends the strength of the Green ray, which is healing and growth, to the heart center, encouraging emotional healing and renewal.

It is often through acts of courage that we find the strength of our own convictions and beliefs. Courage is the ability to act, even in situations that threaten the very life force of the body, because of a conviction of higher truth. Bloodstone calls one forth from the shadows of uncertainty, and aids one in stepping upon the path of courage.

Courage does not mean stepping needlessly into danger or difficulty, or taking unnecessary risks to prove your 'bravery' to others. True courage is the strength of mind and spirit needed to take the action that is dictated to you by your heart. This is the path of the spiritual warrior.

Bloodstone calls this courage forth, enabling you to manifest your personal truth and your heart's desires upon the Earth plane.

THE MESSAGE

Bloodstone has appeared at this time to encourage (inspire with courage) you to recognize the direction in which your heart is leading you. This physical world is a school, a play that we are acting out with the others around us. At any time we can rewrite or change the script. This is how you create your own reality. Sometimes fear of censure, fear of loss, or fear of failure can keep you from following your dreams.

Bloodstone has come to lend you courage so that you can hear the direction your heart calls from, and take your first steps toward it. Bloodstone walks beside you as you set foot upon your path as a spiritual warrior.

CHAKRA: Root and Navel
AFFIRMATION: I have the courage to act
upon my inner guidance.

PROSPERITY

GARNET

GARNET

PROSPERITY

In a fertile garden, a golden vessel full of new wine sits next to a cornucopia flowing with fruit and riches. Garnet is the stone of fertility, abundance, prosperity and Earth power. It is through our first or root chakra that we receive energy from the great Earth Mother. Garnet is a powerful Ally in the establishment and activation of the connecting cord that links us to this element. It is through this cord that we can both receive sustenance from the Earth and offer her our own Light and energy, bringing us back into balance with the being on which we live.

Garnets carry an enriching and nourishing energy. They not only encourage the flow of energy between the Earth and the humans who utilize them, but also act as powerful cleansers and activators of the first chakra, initiating the Kundalini flow and an ecstatic fusing with the expression of All That Is on the Earth plane.

Garnets initiate the remembrance that all life is interconnected and springs from the same source. Seeing the divine in all creation, and re-experiencing the limitless nurturing and provision of the Universe are just two of the wonderful side effects of resonating with this powerful Ally.

The rich colours of Garnet stones remind us of the abundance, prosperity, and plenty that the Earth Mother offers to us, if we will open ourselves to receiving them. Garnet tells us that we have sprung from the blood and bones of this Earth, and reminds us that the Earth Mother will provide us with all that we need.

Garnet's energy is the balancing polarity of Ruby. While Ruby represents the will to survive, Garnet carries the knowledge that all needs will be provided for. When these two energies are in balance, we are able to ask the Universe for what we need, and recognize the solution when it appears.

The Universe is an unlimited resource of energy, supplying you with whatever you need. When you create abundance in your life, you are showing others that it is possible, and that prosperity is available to everyone. Garnet is calling you to remember your own worth. It has come as a messenger to remind you that you are an unlimited child of the Creative source. Whatever you ask, you shall receive.

THE MESSAGE

When Garnet appears in your cards, it is reminding you to open your eyes to the bounty and prosperity that is being offered to you by the Universe. The Earth is the perfect vehicle for providing you with all that you could need to survive and thrive in physical form. Ask for what you need, and acknowledge that this, or something even better, will be given to you.

The illusion of scarcity was created by humanity as an outgrowth of the illusion of separation. In truth, there is enough prosperity and wealth to ensure that every human's needs are met. It is only through your own ideas of scarcity that you staunch the flow of prosperity into your life. When you accept the prosperity of the Universe, you are able to bear witness to the bounty of your birthright as a child of the Divine Creator.

Garnet is calling you to accept the gifts that have been set before you. Acknowledge those that you have received with gratitude, and affirm your belief in a prosperous and bountiful Universe for all beings.

CHAKRA: Root
AFFIRMATION: I receive abundance
through all channels of the Universe.

GROUNDING

SMOKEY QUARTZ

ʃMOKEY QUARTZ

GROUNDING

At the end of a box canyon, a Smokey Quartz crystal stands sentinel over the well of Earth energy. Through connection with the Earth by means of the practice of grounding, one is able to access an almost limitless supply of energy. This well of energy will not only supply your needs, but will also accept and clear energies that no longer serve.

Smokey Quartz is Quartz that has been exposed to a natural source of radiation from the Earth. This exposure turns the stone to a beautiful smokey brown. Because it has been permeated with the strong vibrations of Earth radiation, natural Smokey Quartz is a powerful Ally in connecting with the Earth. When we resonate in harmony with the planet, the energetic cord that links our Earth Star and first chakras becomes activated. This enhances our ability to both receive energy from the Earth, and channel excess energies into the Earth. This state of energetic symbiosis with the planet is called "grounding".

Grounding is an important state of being for the Lightworker. Without the capacity to ground energies into the Earth through this cord, our own energy systems develop stagnation. Without this vital connection to the Earth, there is nowhere for excess energy to go, and so the flow of energy within our body slows. We are no longer able to bring energy in through our chakras, and blockages develop that inhibit our ability to function in physicality. We become isolated from both the realm of physicality and the realm of Spirit.

Smokey Quartz allows us to reconnect with our planet, enabling us to "give away" excess energy to the Earth, so that she can utilize it for her purposes. The process of grounding also allows us to move into resonance with the Earth more easily. This enables us to replenish our stores of energy when they are depleted. The process of grounding reestablishes the vital flow of Light frequencies between the physical and spiritual aspects of ourselves, and enables us to become emissaries for the Light on the physical plane.

Smoke is a purifying force that has been used by many ancient cultures to clear and energize sacred space. The energy of Smokey Quartz operates along these lines as well. The vibration of this ally purifies the energies that are shared between the human and the Earth, consecrating this union and making it sacred. Its energy removes the illusion of separation between the spiritual and the physical, allowing us to reunite the kingdoms of Heaven and Earth through the blending of these energies within our own bodies, minds and spirits.

THE MESSAGE

Smokey Quartz has come to gently remind you that you need to reconnect with the Earth upon which you live. You have chosen the Earth plane as your home for this lifetime, and though you may long for the return to the freedom of your energetic state of being, you must remember that you have a task to complete before you can return to those higher realms of energy.

It is extremely difficult to act on the Earth plane when your head is in the clouds, and unless you bring that high energy down and share it with the Earth, your energy will become stagnant, and your higher chakras will close. You will be unable to fulfill the purpose that you took upon yourself when you incarnated into the physical realm.

Smoky Quartz has come to aid you in entering into communion with the Earth, and reopening yourself to the gifts and lessons of the Earth plane. Accept the gift of knowledge that the physical experience is offering you. Birth your purpose into the Earth plane, expressing your higher Light through the physical realm. It is through this expression of Light in the physical world that you will fulfill your service and create joy on Earth.

CHAKRA: Earthstar and Root
AFFIRMATION: I am a channel for Spirit on Earth.

BEGINNINGS

PETRIFIED WOOD

Petrified Wood

Beginnings

Under the roots of an ancient grandmother tree is the source of the Universe. This is the image of "Beginnings".

Petrified Wood is a mineral, usually Agate, that has replaced the wood of ancient fossilized trees, retaining their shape, texture, and even their growth ring pattern. Trees are the chieftains of the Plant kingdom, towering above the Earth with their roots sunk deeply into the ground. Trees sing to the wind and the sun, and learn much of other beings by offering them shelter, food, and safety.

Trees symbolize the deep and ancient beginnings of all things. On their Earth walk they learn much of the beginnings and endings within the spiral of life. They grow from the seeds of their forefathers, and fertilize their children with their bodies when they depart. When trees become fossilized and have 'turned' to stone, the knowledge and understanding of these beings is preserved in the energy patterning of the stone that has taken their form.

All of us have our roots or beginnings. When we become incarnate and enter the physical world we choose our parents, our culture, and the ancient memories of our ancestors that will be stored in the DNA of our bodies. It is with these choices that we form the basis for our physical experience. The energy of Petrified Wood enables us to access those beginnings, which are stored on a cellular level and draw strength and knowledge from our ancestors and our lineage.

By exploring the roots and beginnings of our bodies and cultures, we can empower ourselves through the ancient codings of instinct and intuition. We can "speak" to those who went before and gain wisdom from them.

Delving into these ancient cellular memories allows us to move forward as well. We are the forefront of a new civilization on Earth. By utilizing the memories of our peoples, we can integrate the lessons that they learned and avoid the mistakes that were made in the past.

This is a time for all people to come together in peace and harmony, without regard to race, color, religion or beliefs. As we move forward into this time of harmony and Light, we will find the ancient roots that are common to all. With the understanding of these ancient tribal ways, we can create a touch stone, a place of common ground, that we can use to build a new life together on the planet. By seeing where we have come from, we are able to move into a brighter future and toward a new day of honoring the Earth and each other.

THE MESSAGE

Petrified Wood has come, with it's message of roots and beginnings, to remind you of the knowledge that you carry deep within yourself. By accessing this knowledge, you can gain a deeper understanding of yourself and your path. You can find new ways of relating with the other beings with whom you share your world, no matter what their kingdom.

As you move more deeply into your own awareness you may access information of your ancestors and your past or alternate lives. Honor where you have been. Your path has given you the strength and the knowledge to be where you are now. On your path you have learned much. Now it is time for you to honor your beginnings, old and new.

Petrified Wood can also herald a time when you will be taking steps upon a new path. Recognize this new path as a new beginning in your life. Release the old and allow this new direction to establish itself firmly in your life. A new direction is being indicated to you now.

CHAKRA: Root

AFFIRMATION: The roots of my experiences
nourish me deeply.

Fire element allies

Fire

The Element of Fire is an intensely powerful Ally to call upon when total and extreme cleansing and change are called for. Fire dwells within the heart of the Earth, and it's mighty force is displayed in it's ability to turn solid rock into molten lava. It's powers of destruction feed the cycle of rebirth and life, as exampled in the legends of the Phoenix and the Dragon.

The legend of the Phoenix tells of a great bird of incredible beauty that was said to live 500 years. At the end of its life the Phoenix would burst into flames and be consumed. From its own ashes the spirit of the Phoenix would fashion a new body, and be reborn into another life cycle with the beauty and purity of youth restored. This legend speaks of Fire's power of transformation.

Transformation is the changing of form, appearance, or structure. In the legend of the Phoenix, the power of fire changes the form of the old bird into ashes, and then to the form of a young bird once again. Through the cleansing and purifying force of Fire, the ancient Phoenix is restored to its youthful purity and beauty.

In the legend of the Dragon, however, the force of Fire reveals it's powers of transmutation. The Dragon is a mighty lizard, with the wings of a bird and breath of Fire. This creature could also live hundreds of years and, like the Phoenix, was an animal of strange and incredible beauty. Unlike the Phoenix, however, the Dragon was a creature of destruction, prowling the countryside and stealing stray animals and people for its meals.

The destruction that the Dragon caused to the flocks and countryside could not go unpunished. Eventually a brave, though usually destitute, peasant boy would take it upon himself to face the Dragon in a heroic quest. Braving the fire and horror of the Dragon's breath, the hero would slay the Dragon, and its carcass would be consumed by it's own inner flames. Instead of turning to mere ashes, however, the cleansing power of the fire would transmute the Dragon's flesh and bones to treasures of gold and precious jewels. The peasant boy would return from this quest a hero and knight, and a very wealthy one at that.

In this legend, the cardinal force of Fire transmutes the evil dragon into something else entirely– in this case, gold and jewels– which represent the rewards given to a brave heart that has survived the cleansing energies of Fire. This legend reflects the ability of Fire to consume one form that energy has taken and convert it to an entirely different form. This is the power that the ancient alchemists sought in attempting to change lead to gold.

The powers of transformation and transmutation make Fire a vital force to invoke for those who are in need of drastic and profound change in a situation. This change is not easily bought, however, and one can expect to learn significant lessons about oneself when one employs this element to create change in one's life. The saying "trial by fire" is not just a phrase, but is an aspect of the spiritual quest that is considered crucial to the acquirement of mastery of the physical plane and the process of manifestation.

The Elemental force of Fire is embodied by us in our second and third chakras, located two inches below and two inches above the navel. These centers are the seat our creative force, sexual energy and will. These chakras are often overlooked or misunderstood in our culture as being centers of "base" energies that are not "spiritual". In fact, these energy centers contain powerful forces that are an integral part of our personal power. Our own will to create and pro-create is an echo within us of the creative force of the Universe. Each of our creations can be an offering of thanks to the Universe that bore us, and a representation of the Light that we strive to bring to this physical realm.

Through invoking and facing the creative force of the Fire within, we can purify our energy, transform our bodies and minds, and transmute our creations into higher and more beautiful expressions of the Light. The polarity of the creative force is destruction, which is also an important aspect of the energy of Fire. Utilizing Fire's power of destruction, we can discreate those aspects of our lives which no longer serve us, and from the ashes we can form new and more joyful creations.

THE MESSAGE

The Element of Fire has appeared an a signal for you to prepare for a transformation! You are being initiated in a "trial by Fire" that will create drastic change in your experience of the physical world. Before the creation of the new can begin, however, the destruction of the old must take place. Fire is directing you to seek deep within, to find the outmoded aspects of your life, and then offer them up to the dragon within, to be transmuted into new and more beautiful creations.

Old habits, possessions, beliefs, and creations that no longer serve you are to be swept away in the flames of your own creative force. From the ashes of these outmoded creations, new and more powerful creations will emerge. By offering those things that are no longer needed to the flame of creation, you are making room in your life for the gifts that the universe is offering to you.

This transformation and transmutation of spirit will be intense. It is through Fire that we become purified and renewed. Attempting to hold onto those things in your life that no longer serve you will only create difficulty. Release them readily, and you will find them replaced with the "gold and jewels" of spiritual growth and abundant physical creations.

One way to aid in this release is through a candle ritual. Carve symbols for those things that you want to release or transmute into the sides of a candle. Light the flame and meditate upon releasing these things to the flame of fire that will transmute them. Allow the candle to burn until all of the symbols have been melted and transmuted into heat and light. Focus upon releasing them to the Universe, where the creative force will utilize the energy to create new and better forms for you.

CREATION

ZINCITE

 INCITE

CREATION

Zincite is an amazing mineral Ally that ranges in color from cherry red, through the orange ray, to golden yellow, occasionally exhibiting a light green or blue ray as well. This mineral does occur naturally in tiny crystals, but the most beautiful specimens are the result of the process of zinc smelting. These incredible crystals grow spontaneously within the ventilation shafts of some old-style zinc smelting furnaces, creating a wonderful synergy between the natural mineral world and the creative capacities of humanity.

Zincite is the Ally that embodies the frequencies of the Divine force of creation. This force has two parts; the first being the process of creation, and the second being the process of manifestation. The energy of creation is the frequency that we generate on an etheric level that creates a framework of energy, or etheric blueprint, of what we wish to bring into the physical world.

The process of Manifestation brings this etheric blueprint into the physical world as matter and experience. While these may sound so similar as to be one and the same, creation and manifestation are very distinct energetic processes.

The process of creation is governed by the second chakra, which is about two inches below the navel. This is the center of energy through which we experience our sexual and creative drives. Sexual energy is the most potent form of creative energy; and if controlled and channeled properly, it can become one of the highest and most powerful energies available to us on the Earth plane. When energy is generated in this center, it leads us to act on the physical plane to express the energy: it leads us to manifest the energy as action or physical creation.

Children use this second chakra energies in a very pure way- utilizing it to experience the physical world around them through the vehicle of the body. The incredible energy that children exhibit comes from having a clear and functioning second chakra, generating an abundance of creative/sexual energy. It is only later, in puberty, that we begin to focus the energy of creation almost exclusively through the act of sex.

To conform to cultural and social norms, we begin to suppress and deny this energy, eventually leading to the blockage of its flow in our bodies. This blockage makes it very difficult for us to experience true creativity. When we begin to feel energy rise in our second chakra, we automatically assign it a sexual role, instead of allowing it to rise up the chakric column and through the higher chakras as creative expression.

Zincite's frequencies clear the blockages that we began accumulating in our second chakra during puberty. Its energies unlock our creative facilities and aid us in returning to a state of childlike expression of our sexual/creative energy. Zincite helps to reawaken the joy of creation that is sleeping within our inner child. It's energy aids us in locating and discreating the blocks that inhibit us from joyfully creating and enjoying universal abundance on the Earth plane.

THE MESSAGE

Zincite has appeared in your cards to tell you that creativity is called for in the current situation. You are a naturally creative being, and one of your roles on the Earth plane is to master the processes of creation and manifestation. An integral tool in learning to create is the energy of your own sexual drive. This drive is the same energy that you utilized as a child to create and play out your dreams and ideas. During puberty, this energy became almost exclusively channeled toward sexual expression. It is time to reclaim this important source of personal power by learning to channel this potent force into the higher realms of being.

Zincite has come to remind you of the joy you once found in releasing this energy through play and creativity. Allow the energy of Zincite to open and activate your second chakra, awakening the creative force within. Breathe the energy upward through your central chakric column, allowing it to clear and activate the higher chakras with it's powerful vibration. By activating this powerful inner force of creativity, you will increase your ability to manifest new ideas, experiences and abundance in your life.

Zincite has come as a teacher on this quest of self knowledge and expression. Invoke the energy of Zincite and utilize the fire of your own being to transform and transmute your reality.

CHAKRA: Root, Navel, and Solar Plexus
AFFIRMATION: I follow my joy to abundance, prosperity and fulfillment

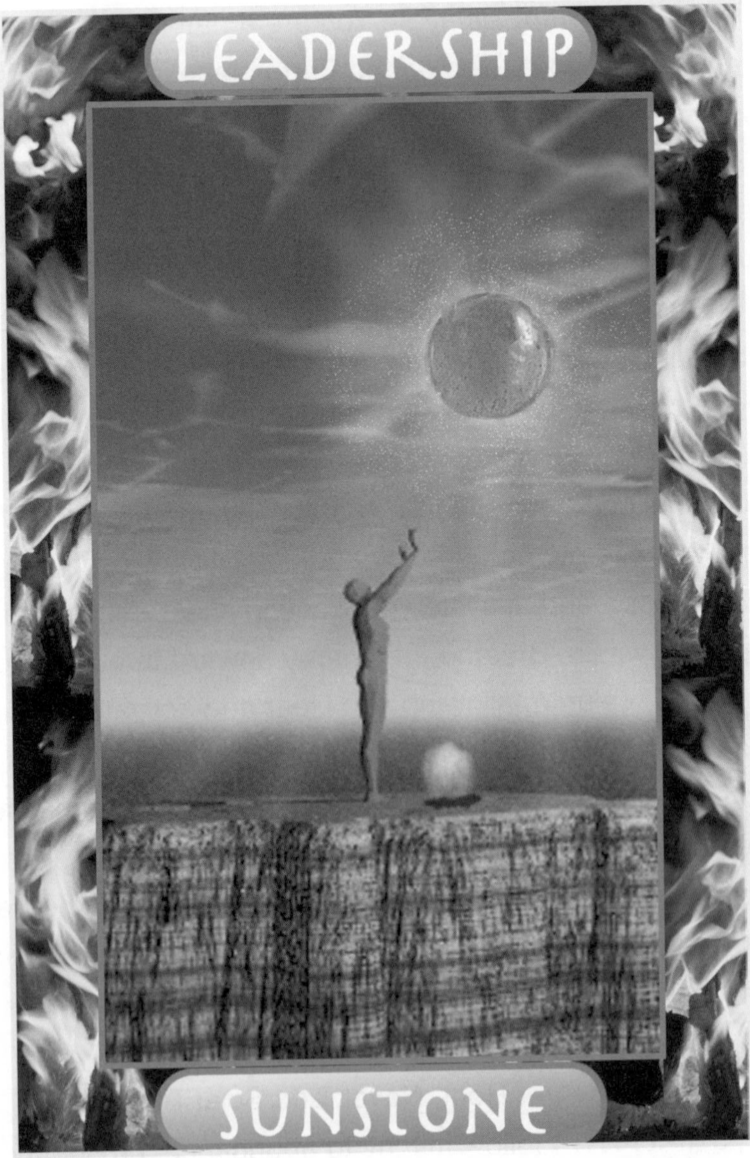
LEADERSHIP
SUNSTONE

$\int$ UN $\int$ TON ϵ

LϵADϵR$\int$HIP

In this image, the chieftain (male leader aspect) of the tribe prays to the sun in order to gain an understanding of which course of action to take. This chieftain makes his prayer in the desert, the realm of Fire energy. It is through the element of Fire that we learn to take appropriate action on the Earth plane.

Sunstone is a variety of oliglioclase, whose brilliant copper-colored flash invokes the energy and power of the Sun. Sunstone is the epitome of the Solar yang vibration, and personifies the energy of the enlightened chieftain of the tribe. It is the stone of leadership, and it lends wisdom in practical and community matters. Sunstone reminds us of the ability of Light energy to influence matters on the Earth plane.

Sunstone is a powerful Ally because of it's ability to bestow clarity in decision making, and the ability to perceive egocentric motives in oneself and others. It activates the second and third chakras, enhancing one's ability to act in accordance with higher knowledge, and with a sense of obligation to the welfare of others. Sunstone teaches us not only of the power of leadership, but of it's responsibilities and lessons as well.

To be an effective leader, the luxuries of self-centered thoughts and ego-based decision making must be sacrificed. One of the great gifts of leadership is that it instills the knowledge of self-discipline, humility, and service, which are qualities that no leader can do without. It is especially important in these times for us to learn the lessons of leadership. If we are to build the Age of Light upon the planet, we must find ways to lead others according to the wisdom that Spirit gives us. When you open yourself to resonance with Sunstone, its wisdom will aid you in learning to walk the path of leadership.

THE MESSAGE

When Sunstone enters your cards, you are being asked to take the position of Leader in the present situation. Be clear about your motivation in assuming this position, as any ego-based motives will ultimately be exposed by the powerful light of Sunstone. Seek out the advice and knowledge of those who have walked further along this path than you have. True leadership begins with the ability to listen to others, and to respond to them from the wisdom of your heart, not the platitudes of ego.

Whatever the specifics of the leadership role that you are to take on, remember that enlightened action for the good of all is the only true course for a leader of today. The power of a leader lies in his or her response-ability. Be willing to take the action the good of all makes apparent to you, and move forward in the courage of your heart's convictions.

CHAKRA: Second and third
AFFIRMATION: I respond joyfully
to the experiences that arise before me.

MANIFESTATION

CITRINE

CITRINE

MANIFESTATION

In this image, the chalice of physicality is filled to overflowing by the abundant energy of the Universe, manifesting in brilliant jewels on the Earth plane.

Much of our experience on the Earth plane is gained from our attempts to transform our dreams and wishes into physical tangibility. This is the process of manifestation– of creating physical form or experience from the energetic blueprints that we create with our thoughts, beliefs, and desires. Citrine our foremost Ally in the process of manifestation. The vibration of Citrine stimulates our second and third chakras, initiating our creative energy and our will, and increasing our ability to make energy manifest.

Manifestation is the second part in the process of creation. The first part is the creation of an energetic framework or blueprint, which outlines what we wish to create. We create this blueprint every moment; through the words that we speak, the ideas that we hold in our mind, and the actions and choices that we make in our beliefs and ideas. We can manifest only what we have created on an energetic level.

When we hold onto outmoded beliefs, thoughts, and desires, we can create blockages in our third chakra, resulting in the manifestation of experiences that do not serve our path of growing through joy. Citrine strengthens the resonant field of our second and third chakras, clearing blockages from our energy systems. When these blocks have been cleared, we are able to create purer energetic blueprints for our reality. This makes it easier for us to manifest those experiences and objects that will serve us more fully on our path.

Our third chakra is the chakra of the will. This chakra can be governed either by our ego, or by the will of the Universe. When it is governed by the ego, we struggle to manifest things that we think will make us feel better, especially those things that we do not need, but would like to have as "proof" of our success in the world. These objects are unable to fulfill our true needs, and therefore, are unable to make us truly happy. The result is a sense of being unfulfilled and unhappy. This creates further blocks in the chakra, eventually leading to a feeling of total separation from Divine Will and Protection.

When our third chakra is clear, however, we are able to use it in receiving and manifesting Divine Will. Divine Will is the force that aids us in creating our highest and most fulfilling path. When we are open to Divine Will, our path of love unfolds before us, creating a more joyful lifetime and learning experience.

Manifestation becomes easier because we are putting our energy only into those things that are guided by Universal Will and Law. There is no struggle because you gain a sense of faith in the protective and provisionary powers of the Universe.

Citrine enables us to open more fully to the energy of Divine Will, and the path of love. By resonating with the energy of Citrine, we are reminded that we are loved and supported in our manifestations by the Universe. Choose the path of love and joy, manifesting that which is truly beautiful by opening yourself to the power of Divine Will and Citrine's teachings of Divine manifestation.

THE MESSAGE

When Citrine appears in your layout, you are being asked to take a good look at what you are creating at the moment. What are the beliefs, thoughts and desires that are creating the present situation for you? Remember, you will manifest whatever it is that you hold most in your mind and energy. Are your words and actions consistent with what you want to create?

Citrine has appeared today as your Ally, in order to aid you in clarifying what it is you truly want to manifest. Open yourself to its guidance and to the Divine Will. Allow yourself to become a channel for the creations that the Universe is sending you. When you align yourself with these sources of higher guidance, you will learn to manifest only those things that are for the highest good of all concerned. In this way, you will begin to see each creation you birth onto the Earth plane as a manifestation of Light, and an expression of joy.

CHAKRA: Navel and Solar Plexus
AFFIRMATION: I co-create in harmony
with the Divine Will.

ACTION

CARNELIAN

Carnelian

Action

In this image, the male aspect of Spirit has come to the end of his road. He must take action in order to move forward on his path, even though the way is difficult and the chasm deep.

Carnelian is a variety of chalcedony that exhibits the brown, red and orange range of the spectrum. It is an Ally whose energies spark action and movement toward our goals and dreams. Carnelian's frequency resonates on the physical level– cleansing the blood, stimulating the creative and reproductive energies, and encouraging us to utilize our physical energies to effect change.

Carnelian reminds us of the balance between connecting with the Divine and actually taking action on the guidance and inspiration we have received. We cannot sit back and wait for the Universe to "do it all" for us. We must take initiative and signal the Universe by our actions that we are truly prepared to do what it takes to achieve our dreams.

The saying, "God helps those that help themselves", speaks to this energy of action. We are co-creators with the Divine; and while Divine inspiration and impetus is key to our ability to create on the physical plane, it will get us nowhere if we do not take the initiative and act upon our guidance.

Another aspect of the energy of Carnelian is it's ability to strengthen and fortify the physical body, enhancing the flow of life force energy, and it's expression through physical vitality. Our physical bodies are the houses of our spirit. When we neglect the physical, we are neglecting the temple in which our spirit resides during this lifetime.

Carnelian's energy resonates with the physical levels of our being, focusing our attention upon the state of our spirit's house. We can strengthen our connection to the Divine by strengthening the physical structure which supports our spirit. Carnelian reminds us of the value of physical strength and health.

THE MESSAGE

Carnelian has called upon you today in order to remind you of your course of action. Seeking spiritual guidance and advice is the first step in creating your reality, but the second and most important step is to take action upon that inner guidance. Without action, there is no creation; and we have chosen to come into this world in order to learn to co-create with the Universe.

Do not fear action because of the possibility of failure. There is no failure, just as there are no mistakes. Each action that you take leads you to a learning experience. Every learning experience that you have adds to the store of wisdom that you can share with others, and leads you closer to your goal of self-understanding. Listen to your higher guidance, open yourself to the path that the Universe is clearing for you, and take a step forward. Carnelian has come to guide you on your path of action.

CHAKRA: Navel

AFFIRMATION: I am willing to create my reality.

MALACHITE

WILL

In this image, an ancient Atlantean priest governs wisely by channeling the energy of the Divine through his third chakra. His staff is bent, indicating that the intellect, not the force of the body, is his guide in governance. The priest sits upon a throne in a temple of Malachite, the ally of the right use of Will.

Malachite is a stone that contains patterns of light and dark green bands. It is a powerful ally in the drawing out of unwanted energies from the aura or physical being. Malachite's true power, though, lies in it's ability to clear the influences of the ego from the Will, aligning the third chakra, and the force of our own Will, with that of the Divine.

Malachite teaches us of the appropriate applications of personal power. We apply our personal power on the Earth plane through our third chakra, which is the seat of our Will. It is through our Will that we manifest matter from the energetic framework that we have created with our thoughts, beliefs and desires. This stone teaches us how to correctly apply our innate force of Will to the situations around us in order to affect change.

We are taught in this culture that one must be either domineering and misuse our power to conquer, or be subservient, and envy the power of others. Malachite teaches us the path of balance through these polarities.

Our own Will is aligned either with our ego, or with the Divine Will of the Universe. When our Will is aligned with the ego, we apply that energy through manipulation, bargaining, and the attempted control of others. While we can create and manifest in this way, anything that is created by these methods is usually not for our highest good. The creations will be empty and unsatisfying; leading us to want "more" and "better" creations in order to be fulfilled.

When our Will is aligned with the Divine Will, however, we become channels for manifesting that which is for our highest good. We release the need to create specific forms, and open ourselves to manifesting that which will help us in fulfilling our purpose on Earth. In this way, every creation that we manifest will fulfill a need, even though it may not manifest in the form we expect. This right use of Will creates a sense of trust in the Universe and a feeling of fulfillment and joy in our creations.

In turning over our Will to the Divine, we become conduits for a higher power than we can generate alone. We no longer feel the need to manipulate others into taking responsibility for our creations; but can joyfully accept our part in the creation of the Age of Light. Our own Will force becomes an extension of the Will of the Divine Universal force.

The ancient civilizations that came before us fell when the Will of their leaders became aligned with ego, instead of the Divine Will. Their royalty and priests began exerting their own Will over those they were sworn to protect and serve; creating slavery to fulfill their greed, wars to satiate their desire for domination, and manipulation through fear to satisfy their power hunger. This is the tradition that our cultures were built upon.

It is not surprising then, that most of us were taught to align our Will with our ego in order to create. We must now realign ourselves with the Will of the Divine, if we are to manifest an Age of Light upon the Earth. We must reject the polarities of mastery and slavery if we are to become true leaders in a new age. Malachite's ability to clear the ego from the Will makes it a valuable Ally for those who wish to come back into balance with the Divine Will of the Universe.

THE MESSAGE

Malachite has appeared today to ask you to take a good look at the way that you are using your will. The force of the Will is one of the crucial energies that we use in creating our realities. We can either maintain a victim role by allowing others to be our pawns of action, or we can take a creator's role and recognize how we are applying our will to create our experiences.

Is your Will aligned with the ego, attempting to create through manipulation and coercion? Or is it aligned with the Divine, releasing all expectation of the form that a creation will take, and wanting only to manifest that which is best for your highest good? Take a look at the current situation. How are you using your will to both create and maintain this experience?

Seek the path of balance and right use of will, and the Universe will guide you to resolution that is for the highest good. When you resonate with the energy of Malachite, its vibration will clear the influence of ego from your creations, allowing you to manifest the Will of the Universe.

CHAKRA: Solar Plexus

AFFIRMATION: I am in balance
with the Universe and it's will.

SPONTENAITY

CALCITE

Calcite

SPONTANEITY

In this image, two golden beings celebrate the joy of life by dancing around a Calcite crystal standing stone. Flowers surround and cover the beings, indicating fertility and joy.

Calcite's frequency speaks to our deepest being of the beauty of spontaneity. The most powerful prayers are those that arise from the moment and are backed by our emotions of thanksgiving. Spontaneous acts are acts of beauty when they occur from a place of love and gratitude within us. When we get bogged down in routine we are often unable to experience, moment by moment, the creation of beauty in our lives. Calcite resonates with that place inside of us from which that moment of creation arises.

Each act of spontaneity that we perform is an affirmation of our ability to create. When you give to others in a moment of love, a state of resonance is created. This resonance with love energy opens the channels of creativity and manifestation, allowing you to manifest spiritual joy.

When we were children, our creative force ran strong. We would draw a picture of love for our parents, sing a song from our heart, or pick a bundle of wildflowers for the nature spirits. Our hearts had not yet been hemmed in by the monotony of routine. When we resonate with Calcite as our ally, we are calling that sacred child to come forward once again to sing, create, and celebrate the beauty of life and spontaneity.

The frequency of Calcite opens the chakras and aids in the dissolution of energetic and emotional blockages. It's energy leaves one feeling cleansed and open, and it encourages the expression of excess energy through spontaneous acts of love and joy.

Spontaneity can be a prayer of thanksgiving to the Divine, through acts of love on Earth.

THE MESSAGE

Calcite is singing to the wellspring of creativity within you. How long has it been since you have created a spontaneous moment? How long since you sang your own song to the Universe? Or drew a picture, just for the joy of expressing joy? All of these things, as well as the spontaneity of emotion between people, can feed your sense of self and your sense of connection to the Divine. Allow yourself to experience your spontaneity again. By tapping into that source of beauty and power in your life, you experience moments of true creation.

What better way to affirm your capacity as creator of your life than by experiencing it moment to moment? When you get hung up on the daily grind and begin to forget where your true joy lies, allow the spontaneity of Calcite to remind you of the true expression of beauty that life can be.

CHAKRA: Navel
AFFIRMATION: I create each moment
as an expression of my deepest joy.

CHILD WITHIN

RHODOCHROSITE

RHODOCHROSITE

INNER CHILD

Rhodochrosite is a pink ray stone that forms both in crystalline and massive forms. It is a powerful heart healer, forming a bridge between the lower chakras of Fire and the upper chakra of Water. Because of its relation to both elements, it has the capacity to cool emotional heat, and to provide insight into issues of the heart and Will. Rhodochrosite's vibration aids in the healing of emotional wounds that originated in childhood, while the will and heart chakras were still forming.

Rhodochrosite's frequencies resonate with the child within. The child within uses it's second chakra energy as a source for unlimited creativity and joyful manifestation. It explores the realm of the physical world with curiosity and wonder. Through our child within, we experience the lessons of total surrender to a higher power. It is through this aspect of our self that our ego developed, and our way of interpreting stimuli evolved.

Our child within experiences and interprets our emotions and experiences by assigning meaning to them according to what we experienced during our formative years as children. Any emotional wounds that we received as children are also held by the child within. Even when we grow older and move on, our child within continues to interpret our experiences through these energetic patterns that are stored in our chakras.

The frequency of Rhodochrosite resonates with our heart and will chakras, allowing old wounds and emotional patterns to be brought to the surface of our consciousness. Once we are aware of the patterns that are still influencing our creations, we can clear them, allowing our child within to release the trauma and begin to heal.

It is through this healing that we once again connect with this aspect of our selves, reclaiming it's innate abilities and talents as our own. Rhodochrosite is the Ally to call upon when this type of emotional and energetic healing is called for. It's frequencies enable our adult self to reconnect with and heal the child within.

THE MESSAGE

Rhodochrosite has come to you today to aid you in connecting with the child within. Is there an aspect of your situation or experience that is perpetuating wounds you received many years ago? This can be an opportunity for you to cleanse and heal any old wound or emotional pattern that needs taking care of. Open yourself to the resonance of Rhodochrosite, and allow its energy to bring any wounds that still need healing to the surface.

Rhodochrosite may also be indicating to you that you have lost touch with the more childlike aspects of yourself. These aspects can teach you many great spiritual lessons as you reconnect with your innate curiosity, creativity, and wonder. Surrender yourself to your higher self and God/ Goddess/ All That Is. Reclaim your childlike faith that all will be provided.

Go within, and clear your energy of old traumas and wounds that no longer serve you, so that you can begin again with the innocence and purity of a child. Allow the energy of Rhodochrosite to sooth, comfort, and aid you in your healing.

CHAKRA: Solar Plexus and Heart
AFFIRMATION: I resonate with love,
and release all else to the Universe.

TALENTS

RHODONITE

RHODONITE

TALENTS

In this image, a female being is creating baskets that will serve her community. Though this is a difficult task, and does not bring fame or glamour to the basket maker, she knows that the true rewards of such work will serve all of her community. For this use of her talents, the basket maker receives the support and gratitude of her community. She knows that through this right use of her talents, she has gained benefits that will truly serve her highest purpose. This is the energy of Rhodonite.

Rhodonite is a pink-to-tan stone that is closely related to Rhodochrosite. Rhodonite works on a deep physical level to aid in the regeneration of tissue and promote healing. It is a tonic for the liver and pancreas, and is helpful in stomach complaints that are related to stress. Rhodonite is an ally whose vibration promotes the emotions of self love and self acceptance. It encourages one to accept one's worth and abilities, enabling one to contribute more fully to the community.

Rhodonite enhances the nurturing aspect of your nature, focusing it inward to support your own growth process. Once you begin to love and heal yourself, you are able to begin to recognize and accept your talents and abilities. In acknowledging your abilities, you are able to perceive your personal power and path more fully.

We are each born into this lifetime with a store of talent and skill that we have been given to be used in the path of service. Each one of us has a contribution we can make for the betterment of the whole. When we share these talents with an open heart, we are fulfilling the role that we chose for ourselves upon coming into this world.

In the coming time of changes on this planet, it is more necessary than ever to follow your heart and your talents. We are each being called to express our own individual gifts so that we can share with joy the tasks that we have come into this life to perform. Each of us has unique gifts that will help us to realize the path of Light on the planet. Rhodonite is calling you to discover your own gift, and to share it with those who will most benefit from your talents.

THE MESSAGE

When Rhodonite appears as your Ally, you are being asked to own your skills and talents, and to utilize them in ways that strengthen your personal power and your community and clan. When we are coming from our center and feel self worth, we are able to truly fulfill our potential. This is not the time for false modesty. If you are being praised for your talents or skill, rejoice in your ability to share them with others.

In this Age of Light on Earth, when we are calling the Light into the void, we must each contribute our particular talent for the good of all. Acknowledge your personal beauty and power, and share it with those who come into your sphere of influence. In this way, we will each move with joy into the New Age that awaits us.

CHAKRA: Heart and Solar Plexus
AFFIRMATION: In sharing my talents and skill,
I strengthen myself and my connection to all that is.

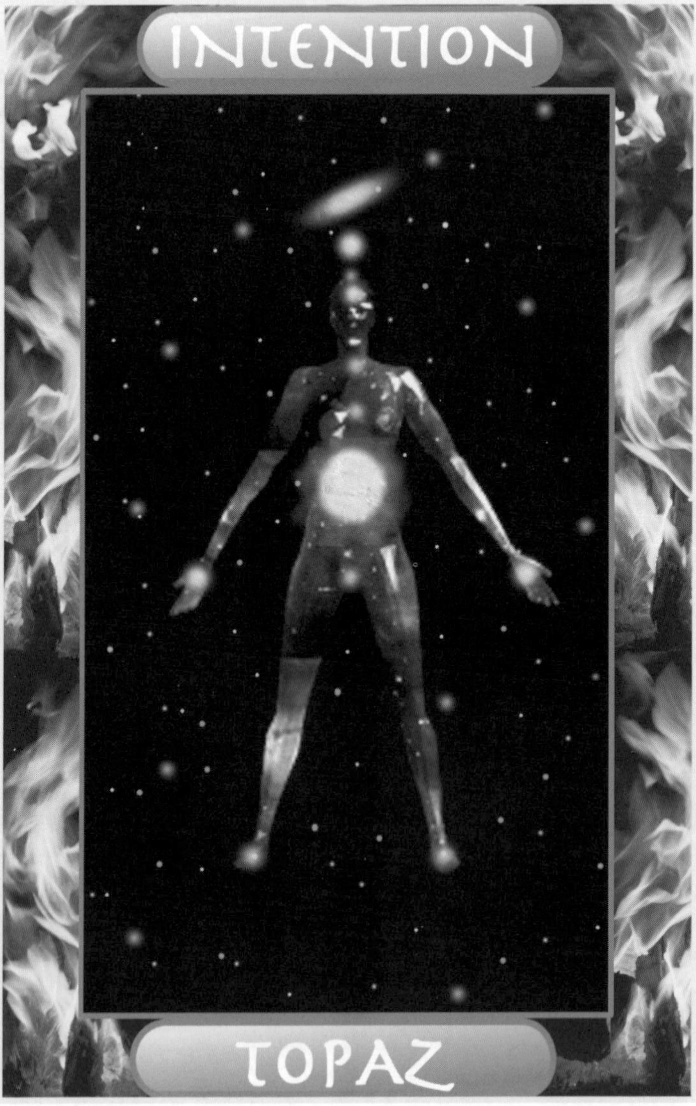
INTENTION
TOPAZ

 OLDEN TOPAZ

INTENTIONS

Golden Topaz, also called Imperial Topaz, is a dazzling golden stone of great energy and power. This Ally has been used for centuries by royalty and others in positions of power because of its ability to reveal the intentions of others. When you enter into resonance with this stone, your second and third chakras become crystal clear and transparent, as do those of others around you. The second and third chakras are the centers of motivation, passion, and the Will. Golden Topaz enables one to perceive and understand the motivations, desires, and intentions of one's self and others.

Intent is a powerful force for creation and manifestation. It is an application of the power of the Will toward creating a specific situation or experience. When we are clear about the outcome of our intentions, what the end result of our creation will be, we are able to manifest more easily and more precisely. By using our intent properly, we strengthen it, just like using a muscle.

But if we use our intent improperly or without discipline, our creations become haphazard and imprecise. Misusing your intention by willfully misleading yourself or others about what it is you wish to create throws a monkey wrench in the entire manifestation machine. It becomes much more difficult to trust yourself or the Universe to manifest that which is good and joyful.

Golden Topaz aids one whose intentions have become obscured, to clear away the debris and reveal the true purpose of your manifestations. By resonating with this Ally, you learn the power of intent.

THE MESSAGE

When Golden Topaz enters your reading, you are being told to take a close look at the way you use your intentions to create your reality. Golden Topaz carries the Golden ray. Divine Truth and its illumination will reveal to you where you need to place your attention in order to create the reality you want. Golden Topaz is asking you to look at where you may be misusing your intention, either willfully or unconsciously.

We can willfully misuse our intention by attempting to mislead others about our motives and wishes. When we do this, we shut out the Divine Light of creation, resulting in confused and unpleasant manifestations. Unconscious misuse of intention occurs when we have deep feelings of unworthiness and a lack of self love. When this is the situation, we create experiences that prove our own self-abusive attitudes.

Either of these situations can be rectified and healed by invoking the energy of Golden Topaz, and learning the true motivations behind your actions and creations. When you become clear in your intent, your reality will reflect the Golden ray of Divine Truth and your true joy will become manifest. Allow Golden Topaz to aid you in your process of self discovery.

CHAKRA: Solar Plexus

AFFIRMATION: I intend to manifest joy.

BALANCE

TIGER EYE

Tiger Eye

BALANCE

Tiger Eye carries a balance of the Solar and Earth energies. It's unique ability to blend these two aspects in one mineral make it a wonderful stone for those who need to attain balance on their Earth path. Tiger eye enhances one's ability to understand and mediate between the two sides of an issue. It is a wonderful ally for those whose profession or path call for this type of balance in judgment.

In our world of duality– good/ bad, male/female, right/ wrong, it is often difficult to remember that the polarities being expressed are simply the two octaves of the same frequency. if you listen closely they do not create discord, but harmony! Once we have experienced the reconciliation of duality, we are truly able to judge without being judgmental. Seeing both sides of an issue as valid, and being able to find the middle way of balance, is the trademark of a true spiritual warrior.

Tiger eye lends it's frequency to this type of balance of perception, enabling one to walk a true path. It is a stone of strength, in that it enhances one's connection to the Earth, while grounding higher energies into the energetic systems and physical body. It is useful for those who are in positions of leadership, as it encourages the balancing of extremes, so that the needs of the majority can be perceived.

Finding our own place of balance is a necessary step for growth. When we are able to respond to the situations that arise around us without losing our sense of center, we are always able to act upon our guidance. Tiger Eye encourages you to find your place of balance within.

THE MESSAGE

Tiger Eye is calling you to look carefully at both sides of the current situation. It may be that in classifying one as right and the other as wrong, you are missing an important viewpoint that could give you insight into how to proceed. Tiger Eye is asking for you to maintain balance and neutrality until you have considered both sides of the issue.

Practice being a witness to what is actually said and done, without running the experience through your personal filters. Allow yourself to be impartial. Perhaps you are being warned against extremes at the moment. Self discipline and self control are powerful skills for those on the spiritual path. If you are considering major life changes now, you may want to fully consider the issue before taking action. There may be a lesson or aspect of the current situation that you have not yet fully learned.

Call upon the frequency of Tiger Eye to aid you in seeing the full import of the situation at hand, then open to the wisdom and guidance you receive.

CHAKRA: Navel

AFFIRMATION: I walk in balance on the path of truth.

Water element allies

WATER

WATER

This is an image of one of my favorite power spots. On the morning I went to photograph this beautiful waterfall, the sun was hitting it just so, and an incredible rainbow stretched across the rock face like a smile. As I sat in wonder-full meditation, my Water Element guide appeared to me and guided me in taking this photograph. Though she is not visible in the photograph, she is standing in the pool that is just below the rainbow.

The Water Element embodies the powers of emotion, communication and cleansing. It encourages adaptability and strength by teaching one to follow the path of least resistance. Yet Water's apparent gentleness is deceptive. Over time, Water can wear down the greatest of mountains, or carve deep canyons through solid rock.

Water is the blood of the Great Earth Mother. It carries nourishment to all parts of her body, and replenishes the land and all of the beings upon it. Water is the cleansing tears of the Earth Mother's joy and sorrow. It is the blood of her menses that form the oceans from which all life sprang. Water is the presence of her emotions, washing, caressing, and nurturing the land and it's beings.

The Element of Water can be invoked to cleanse and purify the aura, washing away all stagnant energies. Though gentle, the energy of Water cleans deeply, and can remove ingrained patterns and traumas from the energy field through the gift of release. Water is a cooling influence, and can counteract the effects of an overabundance of Fire energy. It is a powerful Ally to call upon when one is attempting to strengthen the feminine aspect of one's nature. It encourages receptivity, and is therefore a valuable energy for those who endeavor to utilize their psychic talents.

We experience the energy of Water through the fluids of our own bodies. When we resonate with its energy, every molecule of Water within us vibrates in harmony with this powerful element. Water molecules are in the air we breathe, the food we eat, and the fluids we drink. We absorb the energy of Water after a rain, when it has cleansed and filled the air with it's vibration. Our bodies are mostly Water, and it is more necessary than food to our survival.

Water is also a wonderful conductor of energy. When we are in resonance with this elemental force, we become better receivers and conductors of Light energy. Our cells are able to better communicate with each other and the larger organism; and our energy systems become clearer and more fluid.

In this Age of Light, when we are becoming more aware of the uses and applications of spiritual energies, the element of Water is an important Ally in our quest for knowledge. It teaches us the value of learning through our emotional experiences and the importance of communicating our knowledge and understanding to others. Water also teaches us that when we are on our path, our lives will flow naturally from one lesson to another.

THE MESSAGE

When Water appears in your cards, you can be sure that a gentle yet deep cleansing of old habits and emotions is on the horizon. The energy of Water can be invoked to clear any lingering anger or resentment that may be blocking you from moving forward on your path. It is an energy of lasting peace, and can be very helpful in the dissipation of fiery emotions.

Water may also be speaking to you of the flow of energy through your life. Are you desperately hanging on to old outmoded aspects of your life? Or are you floating peacefully along with the current, trusting that the Universe will deliver you to a better shore? Is your life the rush and fury of white water rapids, or the peaceful eddy of a deep and serene pool? If you watch a stream closely, you will see that there is always a balance between the rushing and the quiet . Call upon the energy of Water to aid you in finding the balance of movement and stillness in your life.

Whatever the situation, you can be sure that Water will aid you now in clearing out the old and carrying in the new. Open your heart and your voice to communicate the true essence of who you are. Allow the spirit of Water to speak through you, bringing the communications of emotion and understanding. Take a bath or a swim, and let the energy of Water reverberate through your being.

LOVE

ROSE QUARTZ

Rose Quartz

LOVE

In this image, a Rose Quartz heart is floating on the wings of love through a sunset sky. The light of love emanates from the heart, filling the sky with it's beauty and energy. This is the image of love.

Rose Quartz is one of the most well known of all the minerals. Its beautiful sweet pink-to-lavender color and its heart-warming energy speak to us of the Universal love that is our birthright. As spiritual beings who are temporarily incarnate in the physical realm, we can sometimes forget what the true lesson of life is. Rose Quartz reminds us that the only lasting lesson is love— and that we have already learned it, and we need only to open ourselves to it's healing truth.

Rose Quartz represents the heart of the Great Earth Mother. It is the carrier of the love vibration to the physical plane. Being a Water element stone, Rose Quartz is able to calm and cool excess fiery energies, such as fear and anger. It allows for the expression and cleansing of these emotions through the release of old emotional wounds. Rose Quartz offers the love of the Divine to support and assist one in opening to the abundance of love that exists around us.

The soft pink vibration of Rose Quartz carries a healing vibration for the emotional level of the heart. It brings the consciousness of love into the Earth plane, allowing one to connect with the Divine source while in body.

Rose quartz is wonderful for children, as it helps to ease the transition between the non-physical and physical levels of experience. When a child wears Rose Quartz, she is able to reconnect to the source of beauty and harmony on a spiritual level, and carry the vibration with her into this lifetime.

Rose Quartz is a very healing Ally, helping to gently reveal one's own blockages to Universal love. All dis-ease is caused by a lack of self-love, which is really a resistance to the idea of one's own divinity. Rose Quartz helps to lead you to see your own divinity, thus freeing your capacity to give and receive love.

THE MESSAGE

When Rose Quartz appears to you, you are being gently reminded that only Love can heal your life and your creations. Perhaps you need to focus upon your own love of self in order to gather the inner strength you need to take the next step forward. Perhaps you are harboring old resentment or anger that is keeping you stuck in your current position.

Or maybe you are simply being given a reminder that you are always loved by the Divine. There is nothing that you could ever do, or choose, or become, that would keep the Divine Creator from loving you with all of the power of the Universe.

Rose Quartz may also be telling you that love of a more physical nature is involved in the current situation. Perhaps Cupid is sitting on your shoulder with a quiver full of arrows, pointing you in the direction of a more earthly love.

Open your heart and listen to its soft direction. Allow yourself to move with the flow of the healing waters of emotion. The trusting heart will be carried to its perfect destination!

CHAKRA: Heart

AFFIRMATION: I give Love, I live Love, I am Love.

GROWTH

AVENTURINE

Aventurine

Growth

In this image, the playful fairy of growth babysits a nest full of glittering Aventurine eggs. In her hands, she holds an egg, filling it with Light and love energy. In this way, she joyfully facilitates the growth of the small being inside its shell.

The sparkling green of Aventurine carries the spring-like energies of growth and renewal to the heart chakra. This lovely green variety of quartz can contain particles of Mica or Hematite, which produce flecks of light within the stone. The green ray frequency creates a resonance within the heart chakra that facilitates emotional and physical healing, and the expression of love.

Aventurine promotes healing of the emotions, opening and clearing the heart chakra, and aiding in the healing of the physical heart as well as. It gently removes blockages to Divine love, and encourages us to resonate with the energies of growth and renewal. Aventurine brings to us a reminder of our inherent right to experience the blessings of health, wealth, and happiness.

Growth is a process of experience, integration, and release. We create experiences in our lives so that we can learn specific lessons. When we have had the experience, we review and integrate the lesson that it contained. Once we have integrated these insights and incorporated them into our consciousness, we can release them, keeping the knowledge and information, and allowing the emotions of the experience to disperse.

Aventurine reminds us of the importance of this process, allowing us to complete each of the stages of growth successfully.

Sometimes, however, we become stuck in one of these aspects of experience, and our growth stops. In this case, Aventurine aids us in perceiving which process we need to complete in order to begin on our path of growth again. Old emotional trauma and patterning is often stored in our physical bodies on a cellular level, and can lead to disease and imbalance. Aventurine helps us to identify these old patterns and release them, freeing us to move on to new experiences.

THE MESSAGE

Aventurine has entered your cards today to signal you that a time of growth is at hand. Allow yourself to open to the changes that are coming and celebrate them as evidence that you have moved on to a new level in your life. Review the lessons that you have just learned from your experiences. Sense the old patterns melting away, and take the opportunity to choose which new patterns you now wish to create.

Aventurine may be calling you to accept the healing that your growth has supplied to you. It is sometimes difficult to see how much we have grown until we try on an old aspect of our life that no longer fits. If you are still trying to squeeze into relationships, careers, habits, or thoughts that you have outgrown, make a conscious effort to celebrate your own growth by ritually giving away these old creations, and welcoming the you that you have become.

Like the fairy of growth, the Universe is sending you Light and love, assisting you in the growth that is necessary before you can experience your full potential.

CHAKRA: Heart
AFFIRMATION: I celebrate my growth,
and release those aspects that no longer serve me.

INNER PEACE

TOURMALINE

TOURMALINE

INNER PEACE

In paradise, a private temple serves as your personal retreat. This is a place in which you can release your tensions and problems, allowing peace to fill your heart and mind. This place exists now, deep inside you. By quieting your thoughts, you can enter this temple of inner peace.

Tourmaline has a high content of the mineral Lithium. This mineral is used extensively for the treatment of manic depression and other imbalances of the emotional and vibratory system. When this high lithium stone is introduced into the energy field of a person, it creates an immediate elevation of mood, a calming of the emotions, and an equalizing of one's personal vibration. When engaged in conscious resonance, this Ally helps facilitate the state of "inner peace".

Inner peace is a vibratory state in which you are able to perceive and release emotional patterns that may be influencing the reality you are experiencing. This release of old patterns enables you to experience life in the moment, without feeling the need to play out emotional habits that were created in the past.

When you create your experience in the moment, you no longer feel the need to judge yourself or others. We become judgmental by interpreting current situations through our own past energetic and emotional experiences. When one is in the state of Inner peace, there is no emotion based upon the past or the future; there is only the present. This freedom from old patterns allows you to accept others for what they truly are in the moment.

Inner peace also enables you to remain more fully in communion with higher guidance. When you are existing in the moment, you are able to make each act and thought a manifestation of the Light. You are able to become a clear channel for the Will of the Divine Creator.

THE MESSAGE

When Tourmaline appears to you, you are being told that the answers you are seeking will appear when you stop living for the past or the future, and begin resonating with the vibration of Inner Peace. It is in the moment that we create and live through joy. By living in the current moment you are able to release the emotional patterns you created in the past, and create each moment as you wish it to be.

You will not find your answers in the future, and you will not find them in the play of the past. You will only truly discover yourself when you disconnect from the roles you may have created for yourself and those around you. This can occur when you accept peace with yourself and the world. Seize the moment and become like Tourmaline; emanating peace, joy, and healing.

CHAKRA: Heart

AFFIRMATION: I live and create in the moment.

FORGIVENESS

DIOPTASE

D IOPTASE

FORGIVENESS

In this image, the polarities of Energy and Spirit join together in the healing of duality. When one is in conflict with another, one is reacting to something within one's own self that has not been forgiven and integrated into the whole. By recognizing that space within, one is able to experience the frequency of forgiveness, releasing duality and embracing the totality of the self and all beings.

Dioptase is a beautiful stone that can occur either in single crystals or in drusy occurrences on matrix. The color of Dioptase is a pure green, rivaling that of the Emerald in its clarity and beauty. Dioptase is the most powerful heart chakra stone available, working on the physical level to heal disease caused by a lack of self-love. The energy of this Ally is a reminder to us of the health and happiness that are possible if we are open to the love and healing of the Universe.

The key word to use when invoking the energy of Dioptase is forgiveness. Forgiveness is the willingness to free yourself and others from the role of abuser in your life. When you forgive someone, you are not condoning their actions, but you are releasing yourself from perpetuating the energetic pattern that has caused you pain.

In every situation where forgiveness is necessary, there is an abuser role and a victim role. You have chosen one or the other of these parts in order to learn a certain set of lessons about the polarities of the dynamic that is being played out. The only way

that you can release yourself from the part that you have chosen
is through forgiveness of yourself and the others involved. This
simply means that you release them from having to play their role
for you any longer. When you have released the other players
from their parts, you will find that the play itself changes very
rapidly.

To enter into the state of forgiveness, you need only affirm, "I
release you from playing this role for me", each time you find
yourself resenting another. When this is said each time the
circumstance or emotion arises in your mind, you will very quickly
break the cycle and release the pattern from your life, enabling
you to move forward on your path. Dioptase has appeared in order
to lend you its power of forgiveness. Each time you say the words,
"I release you", you are invoking the power of Dioptase in order to
create change in your life.

THE MESSAGE

Dioptase has appeared to tell you that forgiveness is necessary if you are to move forward on your path. There is a lingering anger and resentment that is keeping you tied to a person or situation that no longer serves you. If you continue with this resentment, you will continue to create situations in your life where you are fulfilling the same role that you have played in the past. It is time now to release yourself from this cycle and move forward.

Make a list of those who have caused you the most harm or to whom you have caused harm. Then, go down the list and say inwardly "I release you from playing this role for me. Go in peace." As you say this, envision the cord that exists between you being cut, and both of you being free to move on. This releases the karmic ties between you and enables you both to create new, more valuable lessons for yourselves. Remember, you are not condoning the actions that have been committed, you are only releasing both of you from perpetuating them further.

Call upon the power of Dioptase as your Ally in this process of forgiveness and healing. Only when you have released yourself from the past can you move into a future of joy.

CHAKRA: Heart

AFFIRMATION: I accept the healing power of forgiveness
into my life.

NURTURE

LARIMAR

LARIMAR

NURTURE

In this image, the female aspect of Spirit is supporting the child within in her arms. In a sea of emotion, the child is held protectively, yet is cleansed of all impurities. This female aspect and child live within all of us, aiding us when we are in need of deep comfort and support. This is the energy of Larimar.

Larimar, also known as blue pectolite or dolphin stone, ranges in color between a vibrant turquoise blue and a pale green. Larimar is found in the Dominican Republic, and it reflects the colors and energies of the Caribbean sea. This Ally often exhibits chatoyancy, giving the impression of waves moving within the stone.

Larimar is volcanic in origin, yet it exudes a nurturing cool vibration that lends itself wonderfully to tempering excess fire in one's energy. This Ally helps one to feel cradled in the arms of protection and love, while it encourages the cleansing and movement of energy throughout the body and aura.

Larimar embodies the perseverance of the Water element. While fire may burn hot, it burns fast, and water can always put it out. Where there is infection or any other 'hot' condition, Larimar's healing and soothing energies can be called upon to calm and cool the energies.

Larimar carries the vibration of nurturing. This energy creates the sensation that one is being comforted and cared for by the Great Earth Mother. Its water energy provides the comfort of the ocean of the womb.

When one is feeling the need for deep cleansing and protection, a water healing can greatly aid in recovering one's sense of connection to the Great Mother. Water healing can mean relaxing in a hot tub to sooth frazzled nerves, taking a swim in the ocean, or even crying, one of the most cleansing and clearing things we can do to release "hot" energy.

As adults we do not always get the nurturing and support that we need. The energy of Larimar is a wonderful Ally to call upon when the need for retreat to the womb is upon you.

THE MESSAGE

When Larimar appears as your Ally, it is calling you to reconnect to the energies of the nurturing, female aspect of yourself and the Universe. Now is not the time for strong movement, but for retreat into the gentle flow of nature.

Perhaps you have been pushing yourself too hard or too long. Maybe you just need a break from the heat of everyday life. Larimar is calling you to cool and soothe your energy.

Drink some water, take a bath, or have a good cry. Then curl up and dream of the blue ocean and azure sky. Listen to the frequency of Larimar in your heart, as it sings you to sleep with the voice of the Great Mother Earth.

CHAKRA: Throat

AFFIRMATION: I am supported and nurtured
by the Energy of the Universe.

SACRED SOUNDS

CHRYSOCOLLA

CHRYSOCOLLA

SACRED SOUND

In this card, musical notes representing the energy of sound float into the sunset, taking on a form and a life of their own as they move out into the world. This image depicts how sound, once it is uttered, gathers energy and becomes manifest in our experiences. This is the lesson of Chrysocolla, the Ally of sacred sound.

Chrysocolla is a blue-green opaque stone that also occurs in a stunning transparent turquoise colored form called gem silica. The frequency of this stone embodies both the clear blue ray of the throat and the green ray of the heart. This combination encourages one to speak what is in the heart. Communicating in a loving and heart centered way is a powerful skill, and Chrysocolla is a powerful Ally when you are called upon to communicate your heart to others.

In this time of change, we are being asked to review and revise our ways of communicating and interacting with one another. The power of the spoken word is now being realized. Chrysocolla has come at this time to aid us in finding new and more balanced ways of interacting, and to aid us in speaking from our hearts and our wisdom, so that we may utilize this sacred power for the highest good.

Chrysocolla also speaks of the power of affirmation. The infinite Universe knows what is in each of our hearts. There is no need to tell it. But words are powerful in creating what we want on the Earth plane. When our words are in line with our hearts and are spoken in prayer to the Divine Light, they cause powerful reverberations throughout the Earth plane, causing change and attracting that which we are praying for. Spoken affirmation is a strong tool for creation and reinforcement on this plane.

The sounds that we make are sacred. The gift of speech is one of the tools we were given by spirit for creation on this plane. We can use sound to create joy and harmony, or to create pain and discord. We can create a loving, abundant world through our affirmations, or we can create an unpleasant and scarcity-filled world. The way that we utilize the sacred power of our voice is a direct reflection of our inner state of being.

Chrysocolla has come to aid us in aligning the sacred sound of our voice with the heart of the Universe, creating only that which is harmonious and joyful.

THE MESSAGE

Chrysocolla is calling you to voice what is in your heart. The sounds that you make with your throat chakra create a resonance throughout your body, energy field, and external environment. Give your emotions a voice through song, toning, or by speaking with others about them. Affirm your heart's desires out loud in order to create a resonance with your words on the Earth plane.

When you use your voice as a tool for expression and release, you open and clear your throat chakra, enabling you to express your highest wisdom more clearly. Chrysocolla has come as your ally in the process of releasing your emotion through sound. Open your heart to Chrysocolla, and resonate with its energy, celebrating life through your sacred sounds.

CHAKRA: Throat and Heart
AFFIRMATION: I use my voice
as a tool of creation and love.

AQUAMARINE

AQUAMARINE

RELEASE

In this image, an ancient temple made of Aquamarine is submerged beneath the beautiful waters of the Caribbean Sea. The temple has long been washed clean by the healing waters, and now contains only light. This is the image of release.

Aquamarine is a lovely blue crystal in the beryl family. This stone resonates at a frequency that opens and clears the throat chakra, facilitating communication and enhancing one's ability to perceive the energy behind the words of others. It is a Water element stone, and so it reflects Water's energy by promoting clarity, movement, and especially release.

The act of release is a vitally important act in the process of growth. The act of release allows room to be made in your life and heart for those things that you wish to create. There is a well known saying which illustrates the truth of the release process:

"If you love something, set it free. If it is yours, it will come back to you. If it does not, then it never was."

While it is important for you to develop ideas about what you would like to create, it is not necessary for you to obsess about them in order for them to manifest. Sometimes, focusing too much upon the form that a manifestation will take can actually inhibit the Universe's ability to aid you in your creation.

Aquamarine reminds us to 'give away' our attachment to our own creations, releasing their hold over our present reality. When we release the essence of what we wish to create, the Universe will provide the perfect form for its manifestation.

Another old proverb that reflects the power that is in the process of release is the one that states that you can't squeeze a fist full of water. The harder you squeeze, the faster it will run out of your hand. It is only when you release your grip, and allow the water to flow that you can experience its true beauty and energy.

The same is true of life. If we attempt to control everything too tightly, we lose our ability to experience the essence of our experiences. It is only through the act of release that we are able to find our true path and receive the gifts that the Universe has for us.

THE MESSAGE

Aquamarine has appeared today as a reminder that it is only by releasing the old that we can make way for the new. Perhaps you are holding on too tightly to an idea or situation that needs to be released in order to take on the form that is most beneficial for you at this time. The Universe will always create that which is for your highest good— if you allow it to.

Aquamarine is asking you to take inventory of your life and possessions, and to release that which no longer fits who you are. Create a give-away ceremony in which you release those aspects from your life; giving away the energy of control, and allowing yourself to have faith that the Universe will use that energy to create what is in your highest good. Clean out your closets, both inner and outer, and create space for the new to take form. Allow the light of Spirit to enter and fill your body and mind.

CHAKRA: Throat

AFFIRMATION: I release that which no longer serves, and accept Universal abundance.

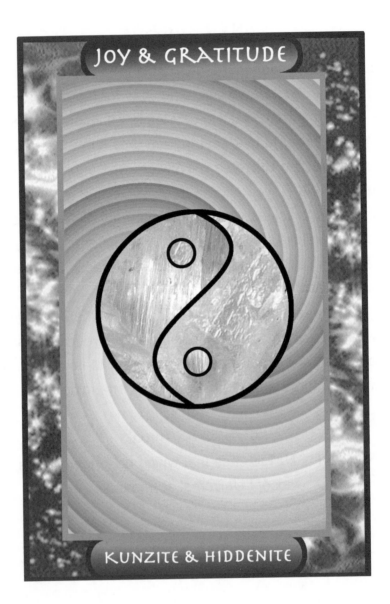

JOY & GRATITUDE

KUNZITE & HIDDENITE

KUNZITE & HIDDENITE
JOY & GRATITUDE

Kunzite and Hiddenite are both varieties of the mineral Spodumene. Kunzite carries the pink ray of Divine love and joy, and Hiddenite carries the green ray of Divine healing and gratitude. Kunzite's realm is the emotion of the heart– learning to see the energy of Divine love in every aspect of reality. Hiddenite is the physical aspect of the heart– the expression and experience of gratitude for the wellspring of abundance and healing that is the Universe.

Joy and gratitude are inseparable. When one is moved to feel joy over some aspect of one's life, one inevitably feels gratitude as well; and when the understanding of the gifts of the Universe stirs the feeling of gratitude within one's heart, it is inevitably followed by joy. The flow of energy created by the emotions of joy and gratitude are similar to a double-helix, the same pattern as our DNA. When we are feeling joy, we are receiving the full energy of Divine Love. When we are experiencing gratitude, we are giving that love back to the Universe. This flow creates an even energy exchange between the Universe and the physical plane.

Though we are but sparks in a vast Universe of stars and consciousness, we are as important to the Divine plan as if its execution depended upon us alone. Many people feel that humanity is a backward and unlovable species, constantly committing crimes against each other and the world in which we live. This attitude, as well as the acts that precipitate it, have their origins in the concept of separation from the Divine force of the Universe.

Kunzite and Hiddenite remind us that when we reconnect with the immeasurable love of the Universe through the emotions of Joy and Gratitude, we see all things as sacred. In renewing our connection to the Divine, we may very well be renewing our chance at the "redemption' of the Human race.

THE MESSAGE

Kunzite and Hiddenite have appeared as your Allies to remind you of the power of joy and gratitude in your life. At the moment in which you experience these emotions, you are experiencing reconnection to the Divine Creator. Gratitude is the recognition of flow between you and the Universe. When you express gratitude for your life and experience, you establish a flow of energy, giving and receiving between your self and the source of all things. This flow strengthens your sense of connection with all beings.

Joy is the recognition of this inner connection. When you sense Joy, you are experiencing the affirmation of the unbreakable bond between the creative force and the creation. While in the state of Joy, you recognize the interconnectedness of all things, and the beauty of the Universe's love for you.

Kunzite and Hiddenite are bringing to you the remembrance of your connection with Source, and the celebration of infinite creation. Be grateful for your lessons, your life, and your creations. Give thanks to the Universe for the opportunity to be a conscious being who is able to learn and grow and change. Celebrate the Joy of being a spark of the Divine's Light on Earth. Share this joy and thanksgiving with others, and soon the entire Human race will be raised up to a new level of understanding and Love.

CHAKRA: Heart

AFFIRMATION: I give thanks joyfully
for the gifts I receive.

PERSONAL TRUTH

AMAZONITE

AMAZONITE

PERSONAL TRUTH

In this image, a mirror of Amazonite stands alone in a vast sky scape. In the mirror is also reflected the image of Amazonite. This is the image of personal truth. That which is on the inside is exhibited on the outside, and is reflected back at you from all that is in your environment.

Amazonite exhibits a perfect blue-green ray with striations of white. This stone's color and energy link it to the ocean, the place of primal creation. When the first life forms appeared in the ocean, a transformation occurred. Oxygen, the breath of life, was created by these life forms within the cradle of the ocean. It is with oxygen and breath that we express our deepest selves and emotions, while water makes up a large percentage of our bodies. The frequency of Amazonite is a blending of these two compounds. Air is water in it's freest form. It is the spirit of water. Water is the body of air. Without one the other could not exist.

Amazonite activates our expressive capabilities and encourages us to speak our higher mind. It encourages balance in our expressions through its own balancing of the properties of Air and Water energies. Speaking one's own inner truth is often difficult. We are taught from an early age to tailor our expressions and emotions to the needs of others. It is time now to take our own emotions and expressions into consideration. We are only upon this Earth for a short time. Who will express your truth if you do not?

Speech is a powerful tool to use in the creation of your reality. When you express your personal truth, you are creating a reality that is in line with the deepest lessons you have come to experience in this lifetime. It is through the expression of personal truth that you gain the respect of yourself and others.

The ability to speak a personal truth is the mark of a spiritual warrior. Call upon the energy of Amazonite to aid you in combining the wisdom of the Air element and the emotion of the Water element. With the aid of this Ally, you will open your heart to higher guidance, and express your personal truth in a way that will serve the highest good of all concerned.

THE MESSAGE

When Amazonite appears in your cards, it is reminding you of the importance of expressing your personal truth through your words and actions. If you live your life according to your truth, you will gain a sense of trust in yourself and your own motives. Your path of growth in this world will become clearer when you cease living your life to please others.

The current situation will not be resolved or freed to move until you have stated your own truth. Have you been hiding your feelings in order to keep from "rocking the boat'? Or perhaps you are being asked to take a stand before everyone, declaring your personal truth in order to make it a reality.

Allow the frequency of Amazonite to resonate deep within your heart and throat chakras, stimulating the words and actions that are living within you. Call upon the spiritual warrior's weapon of personal truth, and know that in declaring your mind and heart, your path will be made clear.

CHAKRA: Heart and Throat
AFFIRMATION: I express my personal truth,
and step onto the path of the spiritual warrior.

ACCEPTANCE

LEPIDOLITE

Lepidolite

Acceptance

In this image, a bowl representing the feminine, receptive aspect of Spirit, floats in an empty sea, with no land in sight. The bowl allows itself to be carried by the current to a new shore. This is the image of acceptance.

Lepidolite is a soft lavender-to-magenta stone with a high lithium content. Like other high lithium stones, Lepidolite creates a calming, soothing energy around the heart chakra and within the aura. Lepidolite often occurs in tandem with Rubellite (pink Tourmaline). This symbiotic relationship combines the soft, calming energy of Lepidolite with the deep sense of love and inner peace that Tourmaline provides.

The resonance that Lepidolite creates within one's energetic field is that of acceptance. Acceptance is the process of surrendering to the higher Will of the Divine Creator. Occasionally, we attempt to force the creation of something that is not in harmony with the Will of the Universe, or is not for the highest good of all concerned. In these situations, the Universe invariably places a roadblock in our path to signal us that what we are attempting to manifest is not harmonious with the Divine plan. When a block such as this occurs, we need to accept the will of the Universe, and 'hand over' the situation to our higher power.

If the creation that you are attempting is indeed the right one for you, the Universe will point you in a direction that will aid in the manifestation of an appropriate form. If the creation you are attempting is not harmonious with that plan, you are being asked to accept that the superior understanding of the Universal mind will provide you with something even better than that which you were attempting to manifest.

The act of acceptance is also an act that nourishes the receptive side of your nature. It is a way in which you can acknowledge your willingness to receive the bounty that the Universe has prepared for you. Practicing acceptance of Universal Will creates trust in the abundance of the Universe.

Acceptance is not the same as giving up or quitting. Acceptance is an act of faith in the greater plan of the Universe, not simply a reaction to frustration and difficulty. In many cases, an act of acceptance takes supreme courage, and the willingness to live your belief in the Universal plan.

THE MESSAGE

Lepidolite has appeared to signal to you that the most productive action you can take at this time is that of accepting the Divine plan. There are many ways that the Universe can work to create miracles in your life. To experience these miracles, you need to recognize when you are being asked to pause and wait for a sign. By opening the receptive side of your nature and practicing acceptance, you are taking yourself out of your own way. Soon, when the Universe has put all of the pieces in their proper places, you will be signaled to take action again.

Lepidolite is telling you to release your present situation to the higher understanding of the Universe. There may be some aspect in what you are attempting to create that is not harmonious with the purposes of the Divine plan. Offer the situation to the Universe, become receptive to a resolution, and accept the guidance that is given to you. You can be sure that whatever purpose the Universe has for you, it will lead you to wonders even more magical than those you could create for yourself.

Allow the energy of Lepidolite to aid you in accepting the bounty that is being offered to you, and know that you are a child of the Universe- joyful, abundant, and Divine.

CHAKRA: Heart
AFFIRMATION: I accept miracles into my life.

WIND ELEMENT ALLIES

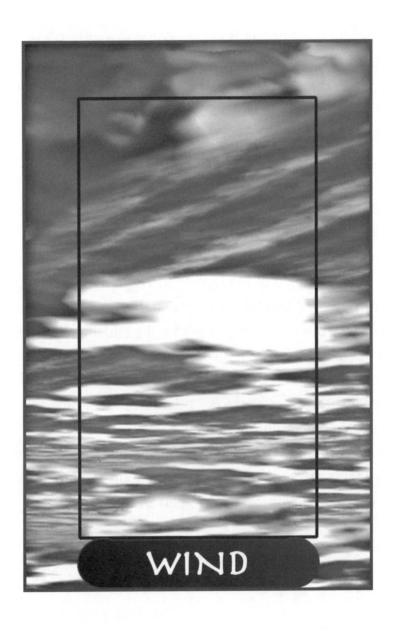

WIND

WIND

Wind is the element that governs the realms of the Spirit world and the mind. It is a force that is capable of incredible displays of strength, yet it is invisible and cannot be seen other than by the effects that it creates. This is like our own spirit, which cannot be touched, but is in evidence through our own creations.

The force of Wind lives within us as our breath and as the gasses of our bodies, such as the oxygen that our cells need in order to survive. Its power is evidenced in the power of our own thoughts to create and effect the reality of the Earth plane. Wind's corresponding chakras are the sixth (third eye) and the seventh (crown) chakras.

Wind is the breath of the Great Earth Mother. This breath is an agent of cleansing for all energies on the non-physical levels. When the power of Wind is invoked, you are calling upon the breath of the Divine to cleanse your life and create change on an energetic level. Through the practice of deep breathing, we can employ the energy of the Wind to clear our bodies of stagnant energy on a cellular level. This element also rules our mental aspect, and it's energy can create improvement in mental acuity and psychic abilities.

The Wind is the messenger of the Spirit world, bringing guidance and information from the higher realms to our conscious minds. Wind can carry thoughts and other energies across the planet, and so It is a useful Ally in the sending of healing energies or telepathic communication over long distances.

The element of Wind is also the force of the Universal mind. It is the Ally that aids us in connecting with our guides and spirit allies, and it allows us to access the non-physical realms of consciousness.

The effects of the Wind element can be as gentle as a refreshing spring breeze, or as dramatic as a hurricane. It can be invoked to cleanse away old debris and bring refreshing change in one's life. Wind's energy is the complimentary force to Water. Water and Air work on many of the same levels, with Water governing the more emotional aspects, and Wind governing the mental and subtle aspects of experience.

The energy of Wind is able to affect change immediately by bringing physical relief to you in times of stress and fatigue. When we are stressed we cease to breathe correctly. This restricts the flow of oxygen and life force in the body, and creates a stagnation of energies. When you find yourself stressed out or in a state of stagnation, invoke the power of Wind to move through you with your own breath. The act of breathing deeply enables Wind to begin it's work immediately by granting you increased mental clarity and energy. Prolonged deep breathing can facilitate a deep sense of connection to the Spirit realm, and can open you to enhanced psychic awareness.

THE MESSAGE

The element of Wind has blown into your cards today to remind you to listen to the voices of Spirit that are speaking. Spirit beings, guides, angels, and your own Higher Self can all utilize Wind energy to carry messages to you. When you quiet yourself and concentrate on the breath of the Wind within you, you open yourself to the guidance of these higher beings.

Wind may be indicating that you need to view the current situation through the higher chakras of the third eye and crown. Perhaps you need to use your mental energies in order to work out a problem. Or maybe you are being asked to open your intuition to receive an answer or new direction from the Spirit world. The energy of Wind may be telling you to "use your head" in the current situation. When the power of Wind is invoked, you are being assured of a renewed clarity of thought, and an increased ability to use your mental abilities to affect change.

Take some time to invite the power of Wind into your life. Sit outside, and breath the Wind into your body. Utilize the power of deep breathing to create clarity and enhance your connection to the subtle realms. Wind is calling upon you to listen to its voice within your deepest self.

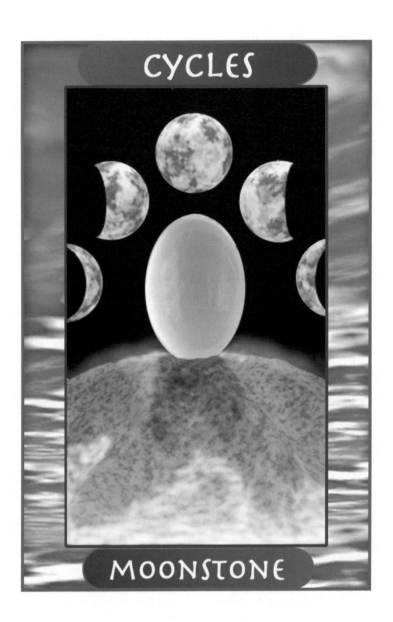

CYCLES

MOONSTONE

MOONSTONE

CYCLES

Moonstone is a stone of mystery. It has often been associated with the feminine because of its ability to enhance the intuitive and receptive side of the mind. Moonstone is a form of the mineral feldspar. It is usually a gray to white stone, though it also can be found less frequently in yellow to peach colors as well. Moonstone is known for it's beautiful chatoyancy, which creates a 'cat's eye' effect as bands of light move across it's surface.

Moonstone has often been associated with the Goddess aspect of All That Is, and its energy has long been valued in helping one to move closer to the Great Mother. When Moonstone is employed by females, it initiates the Kundalini energy and promotes the psychic ability of clairvoyance. When utilized by males, it stimulates the right side of the brain, encouraging non-linear thinking and emotional balance. In both sexes its frequency aids in clearing the aura, activating the sixth and seventh chakras, and activating the central chakric column of energy.

Moonstone has been used for centuries to connect to the energy and power of the moon. The moon plays a vital role in the health of the Earth Mother. Her tides and rhythms are governed by the pull and release of Moon Woman. The energies of the moon affect people as well. The term "lunatic" is derived from the base word "luna" or moon. The cycles of the moon have a strong affect on the physical beings that inhabit the Earth.

The frequency of Moonstone encourages us to pay attention to the cycles in our lives. Each cycle that we complete takes us one level higher on the great spiral. With each cycle our wisdom, understanding, and self knowledge is increased. Moonstone asks us to celebrate the milestones and rights of passage that each new cycle brings. Just as the Moon herself grows full and wanes, so too do aspects of our lives.

THE MESSAGE

When Moonstone shines her beauty upon you, you are being asked to reflect upon the movement in your life. In the situation you are considering, what part of the great cycle are you in at the moment? Are you at the beginning/planting stage, when a seed is just being set? Or has the seed already grown into a young plant, which you are nurturing and helping to grow? Or are you at the harvest, when the fruit has come and is ready to be gathered? Perhaps you are moving into a fallow period, when you are resting and integrating what you have learned from the other cycles?

Everything within our lives has its cycle. Attempting to reap what you have just sown is not realistic. There needs to be a period of growth before the fruit can come to harvest. Alternately, when you really need time to turn inward and rest, attempting to plant and grow a new aspect of your life is not fruitful. Moonstone is calling you to explore which part of the cycle you are currently in, and to take the appropriate action.

Both Moonstone and the Wind element are telling you to honor the current cycle of your life, so that you can live more fully through joy.

CHAKRA: Sixth
AFFIRMATION: I move through the cycles of my life
with joy and acceptance.

DIVINE
CONNECTION

AMETHYST

 AMETHYST

DIVINE CONNECTION

In this image, an Amethyst lotus flower supports the spirit of a meditating being. The energy of the stone clears the crown chakra, allowing the being to draw Light energy and Divine guidance into her energy systems.

Amethyst is one of the most beautiful members of the quartz family. It's clear purple ray has been admired for its beauty and power for centuries. Purple is the ray of the the Divine mind, and royalty have traditionally used the color purple to symbolize their role as the embodiment of the will of the divine. Amethyst is the Ally that represents the higher mind and its manifestation in divine guidance.

Amethyst facilitates connection to your guides and Angels, allowing the sixth and seventh chakras to become open and energized. The frequency of this Ally stimulates psychic abilities and mental functions; it also counteracts the effects of drugs and alcohol, gently aiding one in rejecting self-abuse in all forms. This Ally encourages conscious connection with the Higher Self and higher guidance, allowing understanding of the spiritual lessons of the situations you have created to become apparent.

Amethyst is the Ally that represents and embodies Divine Connection. We cultivate our connection to the Divine by acknowledging and acting upon the guidance that we are given by our higher voices. Amethyst reminds one that asking for Divine Guidance is only the first step.

Trusting one's guidance enough to act upon it is the crucial next step that many of us do not follow through on.

When a friend does not listen to you, you will stop speaking of important things to that person, assuming that they do not value what you have to say. It is the same on a universal level. If you do not value the guidance that you receive from Divine sources, those sources will cease to communicate with you. You can show your willingness to grow by acting upon the inner guidance that you receive through your Divine connection.

THE MESSAGE

When Amethyst enters your cards your Higher Self is sending you a message. Be alert for opportunities, messages, or signs that may indicate the direction your Higher Self and highest guides are preparing for you. These signs may come in the form of intuition, a hunch, or a 'gut feeling'. Perhaps a new book, relationship, or job may be coming your way that will take you further down your path. Whatever the means, you are being sent a wake-up call, and a message to prepare for the working of the Divine in your life.

Amethyst may also be telling you that you are entering into a new state of Divine Connection. By opening to and acting upon guidance and intuition that you receive, you are cultivating a relationship with the Higher mind. Amethyst has come to aid you in creating a firm connection with Higher levels of consciousness. This Ally's energy will help to stimulate your innate psychic abilities, so that you can become a true channel for the Divine to manifest in your life. Open yourself to the energies of Amethyst, and prepare to manifest a new relationship with All That Is.

CHAKRA: Crown chakra

AFFIRMATION: I am open to divine guidance.

MAGIC

LABRADORITE

LABRADORITE

MAGIC

Labradorite is a feldspar that is opaque to translucent, with a blue-gray to rainbow colored chatoyancy. It is a beautiful stone, calling to mind storm clouds and rainbows. Labradorite is a stone used for earth magic and divination. Despite its dark outer appearance, it holds within its darkness a rainbow of brilliant hues that can only be seen when the stone is held in the light. This effect mirrors the energy of this Ally, which enables the Lightworker to work with the unseen realms while purifying her energy in the Light.

Labradorite is a stone of strength and dualities. It acts as an Ally for those who desire to enter the void to gain information and knowledge of the unseen aspects of life. For Shamans and magicians it is a protective and powerful stone that aids in the recall of experiences that one has had in other realms and other lives.

Labradorite creates a force field throughout the aura, protecting and strengthening the energies within and preventing others from "tapping in" to your personal energy and draining you. It can be used as a balancing agent for those who wish to incorporate all of the elements into their energies. Labradorite is an important Ally to invoke when working with Elemental Allies, as it aids one in invoking those nature energies when there is a sincere desire to communicate with nature spirits.

The subtle workings of our inner selves and higher guides are often termed "magic" in our culture. The wonderful synchronicities and opportunities that arise when we are in harmony with all of our aspects create a sense of larger movement in our lives. Labradorite reflects this sense of mystery and wonder, and creates a resonance between all aspects of our selves, enabling our total energy to work in harmony with our Divine purpose. When we are in line with our Divine purpose, our destiny unfolds before us, revealing never before considered ideas and paths to follow.

The energy of Labradorite also aids one in penetrating the veils of the Void, where all knowledge and all possibility are held. The Void is the place of all potential, and is the source of all creation. Labradorite aids the Lightworker in accessing this place of potential, and bringing into this realm those creations which are for the highest good of all beings.

THE MESSAGE

When Labradorite appears as your Ally, it is calling you on a journey inward. The great mystery is about to open before you, and it is time to own what it is you have created. Take a look at the beauty of your life and your spiritual path. Even those things that have seemed dark and dreary are now revealed to contain bits of Light, like the energy of the rainbow.

Labradorite is here to remind you of the magic that is at work in your life. The subtle currents of energy that are shaping your present and future have created something wonderful for you that is just about to be revealed. Magic is becoming visible to you now. It is like a shining, shimmering dew that illuminates all it touches. Take a look at the paths and choices before you. Which seem to sparkle or shimmer in your mind's eye? That may be the path of magic leading you to your dreams!

CHAKRA: Sixth

AFFIRMATION: I am open to the mystery
of the Universe and all of the gifts it holds for me.

INSIGHT

AZURITE

ZURITE

INSIGHT

The inner eye hovers above the mirror of the unconscious in this card's image. With the energy of Azurite, one is able to penetrate the veil, and gain insight into oneself and others. Azurite is a beautiful dark blue stone that occurs in clusters or in single blade-like formations, often with Malachite. This Azure stone is an activator for the third eye chakra, and is known for its ability to stimulate psychic ability and Insight. It clears and opens the third eye, allowing for more conscious use of one's intuitive abilities. Azurite is a powerful Ally for enhancing the psychic senses of deep perception and intuitive understanding.

Insight is the ability to perceive the true nature or motives of a situation or person. When one can see beyond surface appearances, one can gain valuable information that can aid one in making choices that best serve one's path. With the power of Insight, we are able to perceive not only the negative motives of others, but their positive aspects as well. Insight allows one to more clearly perceive others as they truly are– Beings of Light .

Azurite's close association with Malachite is mutually enhancing. Azurite's power of Insight and perception, coupled with Malachite's teachings of the right use of personal and Divine Will, form one of the basic lessons of humanity at this time. We are now working toward correcting the abuses of power that have occurred in the past. As we become more open to our own intuition and insight, and as we apply that insight for the good of all through the right use of Will, we will fulfill our potential as human beings, and can begin the next level of ascent toward Spirit and the evolution of humanity.

Azurite's ability to stimulate inner sight is also useful for the spiritual warrior. As spiritual warriors, we must constantly monitor our own thoughts and motives in an effort to better ourselves mentally, physically and spiritually. For humans, the ego is often a driving force in our motives and actions. Azurite lends us the inner sight to perceive where our motives are based. Are we acting from a spiritual base, or from ego? The spiritual warrior will use her intuitive abilities and inner sight for the highest good of all beings.

THE MESSAGE

Azurite has appeared in your cards to signal you that you are to utilize your insight to perceive the true nature of the situation at hand. There may be something that you have been missing because you continue to look at the surface of the issue. Turn your energy within and invoke the power of Azurite to help you to penetrate the surface of the issue and see the foundations that are creating and maintaining it.

Azurite urges you to allow your intuition to guide you. Close your physical eyes and see with your mind's eye. Azurite is telling you to become aware of the subtle levels of energy at work, and to open yourself to guidance on how to proceed.

Perhaps there is someone that is trying to "pull the wool over your eyes" or to "keep you in the dark". Azurite will act as your spiritual flashlight, shining it's illumination and insight wherever you focus your attention.

CHAKRA: Fifth
AFFIRMATION: I am guided to perceive
the true nature of reality.

JOURNEY

SODALITE

$\int$ ODALITE

JOURNEY

A Sodalite road stretches before the seeker. The road is not easy, and will require courage and stamina to travel, yet it offers many beautiful views and rewards along the way. This is the power of the journey.

I seek, therefore I am. This is the message of Sodalite. This beautiful blue Ally brings to us the reminder that it is the journey, not the destination, that is most important to our growth. Since the beginning of creation we have been driven to explore our world, our thoughts, and each other, in an attempt to discover who we truly are and why we exist. This journey of discovery is the realm of the Ally Sodalite.

Sodalite activates the third eye and mental realms, aiding us in seeing the mile posts along the path of our journey. As we walk this path through life we experience many valuable lessons. Sodalite's frequency strengthens our ability to perceive the lesson at the heart of the experience, so that we can acknowledge the teaching and move on. Sodalite's energy also enables us to gain access to the Akashic records, the etheric library where every person's path is recorded and stored.

When we focus upon the future or the past instead of the moment, we become stressed out, upset and unhappy, always thinking about what is to come, or what has been. When we focus upon the journey, we are placing our attention in the moment. What are you experiencing and creating right now?

What are the patterns, beliefs, and desires that you are living with at the moment? These are road signs along your path that indicate what may be coming. Are you headed in the direction you want to be going in? Only you can decide where your journey takes you, and in each moment you can choose to continue the path you are treading, or change your course.

Sodalite also reminds us that we are on a larger journey as well. It is not only the courses of our own life that we are pursuing. By choosing to be born into this time, we are also choosing to affect the total journey of humanity. Each decision and effort we make along our own path affects the whole as well. We alone can decide if humanity will take the path of growth and change, or fall along the wayside of stagnation and extinction.

THE MESSAGE

Sodalite is signaling you to begin a journey. It is time to take stock of where you have been, where your choices have led you, and where you want to go. Then, set foot upon the path and begin to move forward toward your new experiences. Exploration and adventure are crucial to one's inner work. Explore your interests and intuition, and go where they lead. Sodalite is signaling you to a new and exciting phase of your life.

This Ally also reminds us that in order to know where we are going, we must know where we are. Perhaps you have been past or future tripping so much that you have forgotten where you are on your journey right now. Sodalite is reminding you to take note of the landmarks around you. Explore and experience this place that you have come to on your journey. Honor yourself for all you have created.

Each moment, each step on the journey, we have an opportunity to create ourselves as the person we truly want to be. Choose a direction, and allow Sodalite to guide you down the proper path.

CHAKRA: Sixth

AFFIRMATION: I allow my inner voice
to guide me on my path.

Lapis Lazuli

SELF KNOWLEDGE

Lapis Lazuli is a beautiful deep blue stone that can contain specks of golden Pyrite (occurring in Afghanistan Lapis). This stone was one of the foremost Allies of the Egyptian Royalty, who used it ground into powder for the adornment of the eyes, and as jewelry upon the body.

This Ally confers great depth of sight and clarity upon the user and, when containing Pyrite, enhances these psychic abilities with the grounding and illuminating effects of that mineral. The deep blue of this stone reflects the evening sky, and the Pyrite flecks throughout represent the energies of the stars and the sun in the heavens.

Calling upon this Ally aids one in initiating far sight, and in communicating with spirit beings, especially those beings who have their origins in space. Lapis is used to enhance one's ability to learn and comprehend, as it stimulates the mind.

In ancient Egypt, the Pharaoh was considered to be God, and the other ranks of royalty were held to be consorts of God. To resonate with Lapis is to initiate Divine communion, endowing the user with God-like understanding and mental facilities.

But Lapis also grants one the gift of knowledge of the self. The greatest path of knowledge that we can pursue is the path of self knowledge. Our life on Earth is an opportunity to explore and learn about our own selves– our motives, ambitions, and beliefs.

The Earth plane is particularly suited for this type of exploration because of the existence of the illusion of time. In the non-physical realms there is no lapse between thought and experience. On the Earth plane, there is often a delay between thinking something and experiencing the effects of that thought. This lapse gives us a chance to monitor and explore our thoughts, beliefs, and desires before they manifest into reality.

Self knowledge is the tool with which we can create a reality that is conscious. Without self knowledge, we are often unwilling participants in an unconscious creation. Lapis Lazuli has come to aid us in the opening of our inner eyes, allowing us to see and perceive our own inner world, from which our outer world materializes.

THE MESSAGE

This Ally is indicating to you that a time of intense spiritual learning is at hand. This is a period of initiation into the 'mysteries' of the workings of the Infinite. When Lapis Lazuli appears, you can be sure that your guides and guiding angels are preparing you for a period of growth and enhanced understanding of your path and purpose on the Earth plane. This learning may reveal to you aspects of yourself that were previously unknown to you. Accept this new understanding with joy, for it indicates a new level of spiritual maturity.

Lapis may also be indicating to you that you need to do some soul searching. Are you living the life you would choose for yourself? Are your behaviors and creations matching who you know yourself to be? Take stock of your inner gifts, beliefs, and desires; then ask for the energy of Lapis to aid you in manifesting your true potential on the Earth plane.

CHAKRA: Third eye and crown
AFFIRMATION: I open to Divine understanding

HIGHER SELF

SELENITE

$ELENITE

HIGHER SELF

Selenite is the most beautiful of the gypsum family of minerals. It forms in clear wand shapes with striated sides and occasional water inclusions. Selenite's crystalline structure allows it to move energy easily throughout its form. Its energy is clear, high, and sweet, evoking aspects of both the air and the water elements. Selenite aids in moving energy throughout the water and fluids of our bodies, encouraging the health and en-light-enment of each of our cells.

Selenite's energies allow us to experience the incredible energy of an activated physical vehicle. When all of the separate elements of consciousness in our bodies are activated, we are able to allow our highest visions to enter our physical world. This is the goal of being physical– to bring our highest consciousness into the physical realm and to use it to create an enlightened reality, bringing all humanity into resonance– first with the Earth, then with the Universe.

Selenite is a doorway through which the vibration of our Higher Self can enter into our consciousness and physical systems. The Higher Self is the aspect of ourselves that is aware of the totality of our being. It exists outside of our physical reality, between our mind and our soul. When we are connected to our Higher Self, our physical body and physical manifestations become direct conscious tools for Divine expression in our life.

We are coming to a point in our experience at which we must return to a state of interconnection and connection to the Divine force and will of the Universe. Without this connection we cannot attain our fullest development . Selenite has come to aid us in achieving this end by bringing the light of Spirit into this plane of existence.

THE MESSAGE

Selenite is speaking of your response-ability to your purpose. It is time for you to take your response-ability, and apply it to the new awareness you are beginning to embody. Selenite above all other allies creates resonance in our energy and body that initiates in us a time of renewed connection to the Divine. Through your creations, body, speech and emotions, Selenite will aid you in expressing the Divine in each moment.

Selenite may also be signaling a period of renewed connection to your Higher Self. The ability to move the energy of the Divine through the vehicle of your physical body is an important part of being physical. Selenite is alerting you that it is time to begin developing the physical vehicle you inhabit, so that it can carry ever higher frequencies of energy onto the Earth plane. You may need to change your diet, exercise habits, or other lifestyle choices which may be affecting your ability to carry high frequency energy through your physical being. Pay attention to the signals that you receive from your Higher Self. They will lead you to changes that are most beneficial to you at this time.

CHAKRA: Crown through 12th
AFFIRMATION: I am a reflection on Earth
of the Divine Spirit in Heaven.

PATH OF SERVICE

CHAROITE

CHAROITE

PATH OF SERVICE

A beautiful path leads you through difficult and dark mountains toward a brilliant doorway to the higher realms. This is the image of the "path of service". This path is not always easy, but is the highest path that we can walk on Earth.

Charoite is a gorgeous stone from Siberia. It is a purple, swirling, opaque to translucent stone with chatoyancy and inclusions of black dendritic formations and golden calcite. The energy of Charoite is very activating to the third eye and crown chakra.

Charoite leads one on the path of Divine service, or dharma. By activating and opening the crown chakra and initiating communication with the Divine mind, Charoite enables one to understand how best to serve on Earth as an emissary of the Divine Light. Because of it's inclusions of black, it directs this Divine inspiration into the lower chakras, so that action can be taken on the knowledge received from the higher mind.

If you have been unsure of what path to take in order to best serve on Earth at this time, Charoite has appeared as your Ally to lead you forward. Charoite does not allow one to deviate from the appointed path. If you have called upon Charoite to show you your own Divine path of service, you had best take heed of what you are shown. Though a stern task master if you try to shirk your inner guidance, Charoite is a very high frequency stone that instills a feeling of peace and surrender to Divine will, enabling one to more easily flow with with the river of personal destiny.

    We are all of us here upon Earth to complete certain tasks that
are unique and important. We can enrich our life and spiritual
practice by viewing every task we do as if it were the Divine task
that we came to perform. When we bless each day's tasks with
this view of spiritual service, we find ourselves living in the
moment, fulfilled and open to the guidance of our Higher Self and
the Divine Will. Charoite reminds us that our true path is in service
to each other and to the Divine Light.

THE MESSAGE

Most of us wonder at one time or another why we have incarnated. What is our purpose? Why are we here? If you have been voicing these inner questions lately, your highest guides have answered by sending Charoite as your personal Ally. Charoite's energy will activate the latent inner knowledge that will lead you to your path of service to the Light.

This Ally's energy will help to open and clear your third eye and crown chakras, allowing you to connect with the Divine and receive guidance on your path. You have within you talents and abilities that are unique to your purpose here on the planet. Charoite is calling you to remember these personal gifts, and find a way to apply them for the highest good, in service to all creation.

When you call upon the energy of Charoite to show you your true path, you are sure to get a speedy and clear answer.

CHAKRA: Crown and Third eye
AFFIRMATION: I am in service to the Light.

FLUORITE

SELF DISCIPLINE

Standing upon an empty plain, with no support available, this Fluorite being holds it's self erect through the practice of self discipline. We do not always have others around to hold us up and enable us to walk the right path. In these times, it is important for us to develop our own self discipline, so that we can follow the correct path, even when there is no one to see us.

Fluorite is a stone of unusual capabilities and talents. Occurring in a rainbow array of colors and forms, Fluorite's crystalline structure encourages order, concentration and grounding, and yet maintains one's energy in a high state of openness to Universal frequencies. Fluorite not only encourages reception of higher guidance and information, but aids in its retention, organization, and utilization as well. Fluorite effects the brain directly, reordering it and allowing for the information and insight that one attained in the higher realms to be applied to one's Earth plane experiences.

Fluorite's energies are both grounding and stimulating of one's higher energies. It speaks of organization, self control, discipline, and the need to apply higher guidance that one accesses during mediation and prayer. Fluorite discourages the common addiction to "spacing out" on higher energies, and encourages the application of those energies on the Earth plane. It aids in clearing the energy pathways of the body, and encourages the Light body to integrate with the physical self. Fluorite can aid those who are sensitive and open to the higher realms to maintain an

Earth connection.

Fluorite's main effect upon one's energetic and emotional systems, however, is to remind one of the necessity of developing self discipline in order to fulfill one's role as a spiritual warrior. The ability to bring the body into line with the mind, and to bring the mind into harmony with the Spirit, is Fluorite's true talent.

The development of self discipline and self rule are crucial in those who truly wish to serve others in the coming age. Self discipline is the ability to monitor and correct one's thoughts, actions, and words, in order to improve one's self. It is the inner strength that is necessary to create one's life as one wishes it to be. It is through this inner improvement that we are able to cultivate the skills and knowledge that will aid us in creating the Age of Light upon the Earth.

THE MESSAGE

When Fluorite enters your cards, you are being asked to review your current practices and life style. Fluorite may be calling you to make changes in your life. This could mean organizing your life more efficiently, making necessary changes in your habits, or applying yourself to your path more fully.

We in the forefront of the Age of Light on Earth, are being called upon to organize and apply in our lives those bits of knowledge and understanding with which our journey has supplied us. If you feel as though you have not applied this knowledge in your life, Fluorite is asking you to make the necessary adjustments.

Self discipline means living the life you espouse, or in other words, to "walk your talk". If you have strayed from the path that you know you should be on, you are now being called upon to step back in line with Spirit. Open yourself to the frequency of Fluorite, and allow yourself to begin to vibrate with its energies of self discipline and action.

CHAKRA: Crown
AFFIRMATION: My body is a reflection of my mind.
My mind is a reflection of my spirit.
I am a reflection of Divine Light.

DREAMS

SUGILITE

$\int$UGILITE

DREAMS

Sugilite is a beautiful opaque stone that grows in massive form and can exhibit colors ranging from pale lavender to purple-black. This stone initiates the higher mind, encouraging direct communion with the Divine, and stimulating mental and psychic abilities.

As an Ally, Sugilite aids one in remembering one's Divine purpose. When we choose to become incarnate, we bring with us a certain set of frequencies that generate specific situations from which we learn the lessons we have chosen. Sugilite encourages us to access these frequencies and discover our higher purpose.

Sugilite stimulates the crown chakra, initiating one's ability to receive higher guidance. Its frequency also encourages one to explore and live one's dreams. Dreams and desires are the forces that shape your reality. If you do not honor them and follow their lead, you are denying the Divine inspiration in your life. By attending to higher guidance and your own dreams and desires, you will be led by Divine purpose to those situations and occurrences which will further you on your path.

Night time dreams are reflections of your inner self, containing a mixture of guidance, emotional releas, and inner exploration. You can learn a great deal about yourself by exploring your sleeping dreams. Daydreams reflect your desires and fancies, and are under more conscious control. Daydreams are wonderful ways to experience the manifestation of your desires before they become physical. Sugilite's frequency encourages and strengthens both of these types of dreaming, offering us a powerful link to both your inner and higher self.

Dreams of all kinds lead us to a better understanding of our Subconscious and Unconscious minds. These inner levels of being are direct doorways to the Universal Void, or place of all creation. When we access these levels of being, we are able to create and discreate situations and experiences on the Earth plane. Often, our dreams will speak to us in symbols, the language of our intuitive self. Through this inner dialogue, we can access guidance and information from our deepest self.

Sugilite can aid in the translation of these symbols into conscious understanding, and facilitate their creation on the Earth plane.

THE MESSAGE

When Sugilite appears as your Ally, it is calling you to place your trust in Divine purpose and follow your heart's dreams. You were given your desires as signal lights on your path. If you have a desire to do something other than what you are doing, follow your inner guidance and find a way to explore your dream. Every event that occurs in your life is a creation that allows you to take a step forward on your path.

When you follow your heart's dreams, you will always have the motivation and drive to follow your inner most heart on your path. This is not to say that you should quit your job today and move out of town. Of course, if this seems appropriate, follow it. But if you open your heart and your life to make room for your dream to take root, the Universe will send the appropriate experiences and opportunities your way.

If you start doing what you love in small ways today, you signal to the Divine that you are prepared to take action upon your dreams.

CHAKRA: Crown
AFFIRMATION: I follow my dreams to my highest good.

Storm Element Allies

STORM

$\int$TORM

The element of Storm is the most transformational of the elemental forces. This force is the result of the synergistic combination of the energies of Earth, Fire, Water and Wind. When these elements combine, they create an energy that is more powerful than the sum of it's parts; a force which embodies the moment of creation and destruction in one. Storm is the T'ai Chi, the yin and yang combined. Its frequencies represent both the point of perfect balance, and the extremes of the polarities.

The energy of Storm clears the air and drenches and renews the Earth. It's lightning fire charges the atmosphere with energy and refreshes the mind. Storm carries the energy of rebirth. Rebirth is not always an easy process, and Storm is not always an easy Ally, but both are necessary parts of the cycles of life and nature. When you are in a place of no movement in your life it is as if you are experiencing a period of death. The energy of Storm will create a rebirth in a new direction through which you can explore your life once again.

The element of Storm is active on all levels– physical, emotional and spiritual. Its energy creates profound and drastic change throughout one's experiences. Storm can cause the experience of destruction, as it tears down those aspects of one's life that are no longer stable or strong. This destructive force is cleansing, as it moves through your life uprooting those creations that no longer serve and enabling new experiences and creations to take root.

Storm comes most often when there is a stalemate in one's life, when the air is stagnant and stifling, and there is no longer movement toward one's dreams. When this lack of movement creates a standstill that no single elemental force can move, the elemental Allies combine to create the renewing element of Storm. This force will sweep down upon you, charging your energy and your life once again. Like Dorothy in the Wizard of Oz, you are sure to find yourself set down by the Storm in a new and unexpected place, full of growth, learning and renewal.

THE MESSAGE

When Storm whirls through your cards you are being blessed with a time of great change and growth. The growth that Storm brings is rarely easy. Ego based beliefs and ideas may be shattered. Old beliefs that were held dear may become empty of meaning. But this difficult cleansing of obsolete energies is crucial to gaining new levels of deeper understanding and growth.

Storm is calling you to stretch out your arms to the sky and invoke the powers of lightning, rain, wind and earth. In doing so you will begin your initiation into the deeper mysteries of your life.

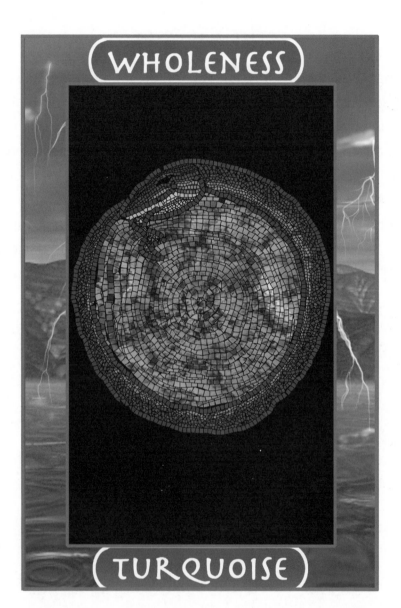

WHOLENESS

(TURQUOISE)

Turquoise

WHOLENESS

In this image the rainbow snake, which represents all creation, contains within it's coils the unity of the Universe, represented by Turquoise. The snake and the Universe that it contains are made up of tiny pieces of creation. This represents the necessity of all creation moving into harmony before wholeness can be achieved. The same is true on a personal level. All aspects of the self must be recognized and integrated before personal wholeness can be achieved. This integration and understanding are the realm of the Ally Turquoise.

This sky blue to green mineral combines Water, Wind, Fire and Earth energies, therefore containing the power and unity of the Storm Element. Turquoise has traditionally been a stone of vision, because of it's incredible sky blue color. The Sky is a male aspect of the Earth Mother. Those beings that inhabit the sky, such as Hawk and Eagle, have incredible powers of vision. Flying hundreds of feet in the air, they not only see the total picture of the landscape below them, but can also discern the movements of the smallest mouse on the ground or fish beneath the water.

Often Turquoise will contain Pyrite, thus combining the male sky energy with the male Earth aspect and the energy of the Sun. This sacred triad symbolizes the return of the wisdom of the heavens to the Earth plane. Part of this wisdom is the ability to perceive the disparate aspects of oneself, and to integrate those aspects into a whole picture of ones total being.

Turquoise symbolizes the marriage of the Earth and the Sky. Because it embodies the energies of all four elements, it represents the escape from the duality of the physical realm and the return to the oneness and unity of the Great Spirit of the Universe. Turquoise calls you to remember that you contain within you all aspects of the Great Earth Mother and all of her moods, which take the earthly form of the elemental forces.

When you invoke the energy of Turquoise, you are asking to be shown the way to Oneness and Unity. By seeking out this path, you are fulfilling the need of the current age of growth on the Earth plane. The Age of Light is a return to wholeness. Humanity long ago volunteered to be the vehicle through which Spirit could learn of the duality of the physical plane. We are now undertaking to reunite the dualism of Light and Dark, Male and Female, Body and Spirit. Turquoise shows us that one can exist in Unity, bringing all polarities and dualism into balance.

THE MESSAGE

When Turquoise appears as your Ally, it calls you to seek the unity within. What is the aspect of the situation that is most difficult for you? This may be the very aspect that you need to recognize in yourself before you can understand how to release it from your experience. Every situation and experience that arises in your life is meant to bring you closer to a sense of wholeness and unity with the Universe. Each experience leads you to a new understanding of yourself and the talents, strengths and weaknesses that you have been given to complete your lifetime here.

Looking within your own heart, you will see that everything you are at odds with in your environment is merely a reflection of an inner part of yourself that you have not acknowledged and integrated. Turquoise is asking you to find that aspect of yourself with which you are having difficulty, and to accept and integrate it into your total self.

CHAKRA: Throat through Soul star
AFFIRMATION: I accept and integrate
all aspects of my self.

Herderite

Evolution

In this image, humanity progresses from being unaware and closed, to an opening toward spirit, finally resulting in the evolution of humanity into human Light beings. This is the energy of Herderite.

Herderite's unique energy embodies the essence of the power of thought. Herderite is a relatively rare mineral whose frequency activates the latent areas of the brain, initiating its more esoteric abilities, including psychic powers, enhanced memory, and other mental gymnastics. These powers are expressions of the Divine within us. When we are aligned with the Universe and employ these powers of the mind, we are activating the new phase of our own Human evolution .

Herderite has a frequency that triggers the areas of our brain that have been latent since our descent in the Atlantean times. Since that time, we have completed a great task which included the exploration of the concept of separation. We are now completing this cycle of learning, and are returning to the level of mental and spiritual ability we commanded before the descent. This evolution of humanity is the completion of a great cycle of growth and learning.

Herderite has appeared at this time to aid us in initiating this evolution of the body, mind and spirit. Herderite's frequency not only stimulates and initiates the brain, but it acts to stimulate the pre-encoded genetic triggers that will initiate us into this new phase of existence. Herderite speaks of evolution in our bodies, our relationships and our creations. By opening ourselves to its vibration, we accept our responsibility to allow deep transformation and emergence into our birthright as human Light beings.

Evolution is defined in the Random House Collegiate Dictionary as: "A motion incomplete in itself, but combining with coordinated motions to produce a single action...."

We are all of us producing single motions every day, through the choices we make, the actions we take, and the thoughts that we have. When we combine those single motions, we create a single action. Each of our experiences and paths, when taken together, create the evolution of Humanity.

Herderite is a unifying force in this action, linking our minds, hearts and energies to produce a single action– Our human evolution.

THE MESSAGE

When Herderite appears as your Ally, you are being asked to acknowledge your part in the total evolution of humanity at this time in history. Your choices and actions are like a drop in a pool, its ripples affecting everything else around it. Are your current motions– your thoughts and actions– moving you toward a higher state of evolution? Or are they ripples of past ways of being that need to be reformed or removed before you can experience your life on a higher level?

As with any Storm element card, Herderite heralds a time of great change. When Herderite appears, it is telling you that this particular time of change is greatly directed by the thoughts and actions that you take. You know in your heart the direction Spirit is asking you to move in. If you accept Spirit's guidance, your actions will cause ripples in the entire fabric of humanity, moving the spiritual evolution of us all forward a step.

CHAKRA: Seventh and etheric chakras
AFFIRMATION: I allow my physical self
to align with my Higher Self now.

TRANSFORMATION

MOLDAVITE

MOLDAVITE

TRANSFORMATION

Moldavite tektite is a beautiful green gemstone that fell to Earth over 14 million years ago in a meteor impact that formed the Bohemian plateau. It is the foremost of the transformational stones in that its energies are felt most easily and it has the most obvious and immediate transformational effect upon one's life. Moldavite exhibits the green ray, yet its energies are effective in burning through blockages in any of the chakras. It is a strong stimulant to the psychic senses, and tends to accelerate one's spiritual development and path.

A strict (some say merciless) teacher, Moldavite heralds a time of drastic growth and changes. People, things or life lessons that no longer serve you will drop away, clearing the path for the higher good to come. This is not always an easy process, but if you are prepared to surrender to the Universal will, it can be a cathartic, cleansing and exciting time of spiritual unfolding.

Moldavite has been valued for it's transformative spiritual energies for at least 25,000 years, and probably longer. Ancient people of the Bohemian plateau and beyond would wear this potent Ally for it's energetic properties. Moldavite is also believed to be the legendary "Emerald that fell from the sky", the stone of the Holy Grail.

Moldavite has an immediate impact on those that attune to its energies. Physical sensations range from the experience of heat ("Moldavite flush") to tingling, dizziness or even headaches.

Don't let this scare you, however. These physical symptoms are only temporary, and are direct effects of the stone's powerful cleansing of the chakras and energetic systems of the body.

Many people also trace the beginning of incredible growth and movement in their lives to their first encounters with Moldavite's energy. Changes in relationships, jobs, living environments, personal abilities and manifestation abilities have all been reported as effects of Moldavite's energy entering one's life. Deep personal transformation is always a part of choosing to work with the Moldavite Ally. Moldavite allows the Light of the Divine to work great changes and miracles in one's life.

THE MESSAGE

If you have drawn Moldavite as your ally, hold on! It's going to be an exciting ride for the next few months. You may experience a "falling away" of old relationships, jobs, securities, and situations. Anything that does not serve your ultimate path may go spinning off into space, leaving you transformed.

Moldavite is not always an easy Ally, as its purgative effects can leave you feeling like you've been put through the ringer, but it is truly a stone that indicates change for the better. It has a beautiful, extremely powerful and high vibration which creates a resonance with Universal understanding and creation.

Expect an increase in psychic or "coincidental" phenomenon. It is time for you to begin the next phase of your spiritual learning, and Moldavite is a powerful teacher!

CHAKRA: Will dissolve blockages in all chakras, but is most active on the Heart, Third eye, Crown, and etheric chakras.

AFFIRMATION: I allow the power of Light
to transform my life.

CLARITY

CLEAR QUARTZ

Clear Quartz

CLARITY

A beautiful crystal rises above the fog and into the clarity of the night sky. This is the image of "Clarity", and it represents the effect of Clear Quartz energy.

To many people, Clear Quartz is what is meant by the term "crystal". Clear Quartz crystals occur naturally in many different configurations. Generally, these crystals exhibit a single termination of six faces joining at the top to form an apex. Clear Quartz is one of the purest and most versatile forms of crystal, carrying a high, clean echo of the Earth Mother's energies. Its key word is clarity, as it's energy clears and amplifies one's thoughts.

Clear Quartz crystals have traditionally been used to aid in the attainment of a clear and balanced mind and energy. This Ally speaks of becoming a vessel for the Light of Spirit, lending yourself to the service of others and living honestly and without deception or deceit. The high vibration of Clear Quartz aids in the cutting through of cloudiness or mental fog, and the enlightenment of the darkness of density. This Crystal Ally is a recorder of the Earth's experiences, and has been used by the ancients as a receptacle for knowledge and secrets.

Because of their wonderful ability to carry any energy easily, Clear Quartz crystals will tend to reflect and amplify any energy that they are exposed to. This quality is wonderful when you wish to employ this Ally as a constant prayer generator. By calming and quieting your mind, then concentrating upon one single thought, you will "program" the crystal with the specific energy of your thought. It will continue to carry the heart of your prayer or thought long after you have set it down and moved ahead in your day.

Clear Quartz reminds us of the ultimate ideal, that of becoming Light incarnate. To exist in form, yet have the vibration of Spirit, is the goal of every spiritual seeker. Clear Quartz exemplifies and encourages this ideal with it's clarity and beauty.

THE MESSAGE

When this stone appears as your Ally, you are being asked to clarify yourself so that the Universe can provide you with the answers to your prayers. Perhaps you have been vacillating between two options. The time has come to choose, and to make your choice known. Call upon the energy of Clear Quartz to aid you in becoming clear about the choices that lie before you. It is through clarity of thought and intent that your creations will be made manifest.

Clear Quartz has made it's spirit known to you in your layout, and you are being notified that the answers to your questions are imminent. Clear Quartz signals a time of deeper understanding of your path. Open yourself to the Divine Light, and allow your future to unfold.

CHAKRA: All

Clear Quartz can energize, balance and clear any of the chakras. It is especially active on the sixth and seventh chakras, promoting mental clarity and concentration.

AFFIRMATION:

I am clear in my thought, intent and desire.
I reflect the clarity of the Divine mind.

HEALING

SERAPHINITE

$\int$ ERAPHINITE

HEALING

Chlorite is usually found as a green mineral, sometimes appearing as inclusions in quartz and other stones. The most powerful form of this stone grows in massive form as a gem chlinichlore and pennite combination commonly called "Seraphinite".

Seraphinite is the most effective stone I have felt for cellular regeneration and healing. On a physical level, it seems to act upon the body like fertilizer on grass, causing a flush of pure healing energy. This stone is an excellent vehicle for discovering and processing physical disease relating to alternate lifetimes. It is a direct link to accessing the energetic structure of the DNA, and the decoding of patterns there.

Seraphinite acts as a trigger mechanism, causing old patterns of disease or imbalance to fall away, and allowing new patterns to be created. It is very useful in aiding in the healing of the heart and lungs, as well as any systemic illnesses relating to cellular regeneration. This mineral stands alone as the premier healing stone of this age. It is the tool most suited to bringing the physical body into line with Light energy.

It is an excellent stone for those who feel disconnected from their physical selves, allowing them to understand more fully the true nature of physicality. Seraphinite's true purpose is to bring light into the physical body, expressing itself through us as glowing health.

We are all in need of healing on some level; be it emotional, physical, or spiritual. The frequency of Seraphinite reveals the underlying causes of imbalance, allowing us to rectify them before they manifest as physical disease. Its ability to connect us to the highest realms of the Spirit while bringing that energy into the physical body makes Seraphinite an important healing Ally.

THE MESSAGE

When Seraphinite appears in your cards, you can be sure that a time of healing is upon you. Healing is the process of bringing aspects of our self that are out of balance back into balance again. Most imbalance is caused by belief in the illusion of separation from Divine love. Seraphinite has come to remind you that you are loved, and that any imbalance you have created can be healed by accepting that love into your life again.

Before we can step fully into the age of Light, we must integrate all of the experiences that reside within our physical body. When we have done this, we can fully experience the clarity of our Light body being anchored on the Earth plane. Seraphinite's frequency aids in the rapid processing, healing, and integration of cellular memories and information, creating clarity in our bodies, emotions, and minds.

By accepting the healing that Seraphinite offers, you can once again experience the beauty of connection to the Divine source of all creation.

CHAKRA : All

AFFIRMATION: I honor my body
as a vehicle for the Light.

SPIRIT

(DANBURITE)

D ANBURITE

SPIRIT

Danburite is a calcium borosilicate that grows in crystal form. When cut this Ally becomes a clear, brilliant gem. The crystals can appear pink, clear, or golden, depending upon the location in which it is mined. This Ally is the stone of the angels. Its beautiful, high, soft energy encourages us to resonate with celestial beings and their purposes.

Danburite is a stone of joy and celebration. Its frequency creates a resonance which allows our energetic field to become more receptive to angelic and spiritual influences. It is also associated with the higher dimensions of love, fellowship and Light. Danburite's key word is Spirit, and its frequencies help to connect us more fully with that aspect of ourselves.

Danburite activates the sixth through the etheric chakras, allowing one to see with the vision of the higher realms. Danburite's strong suit is its ability to reveal to us that which has an energy that is normally too high for us to perceive. Fairies, angels and Light beings of all kinds are made visible with the aid of Danburite's influence. It allows one to 'pierce the veil' that separates us from the Divine in one another.

Danburite is an Ally that represents the realm of the Spirit in physical form. The physical realm that we inhabit is merely a shadow of the greater unseen reality that exists alongside us. Often, the unseen forces that guide us are the most powerful allies in our lives.

Danburite's frequency allows us to perceive the unseen world more fully, and integrate it into our conscious experience through our Light body or aura. The high love energy of Danburite reflects the love of the Universe, initiating within us a resonance and remembrance of the source.

THE MESSAGE

Danburite's sweet energy is calling you to open your eyes to the magic and wonder around you. Fairies are playing in the grass, Light beings are floating through the forest, and the world is full of unseen guides and teachers that are waiting for you to perceive them. If you reach out with your heart and mind to those on the other side, they will respond by offering guidance, love and fun! Seek the unseen, and develop your faith that it is there, hiding, just beyond the veil.

Danburite is asking you to accept the unseen aspects of yourself as well. Close your eyes and explore the extent of your energy. Try picturing everything in your world as your creation, an extension of your thoughts and intent. Acknowledge that the unseen thoughts you think, the emotions you feel, and the desires you have, all affect the world around you. Call upon the energy of Danburite, and the power of your spirit will be made clear to you.

CHAKRA: Third eye, Crown, and Etheric.
AFFIRMATION: I am an infinite part
of an infinite Universe.

INNER BRIDGES

(KYANITE)

KYANITE

INNER BRIDGES

In this image, a bridge of Kyanite spans a tranquil stream, uniting the separate banks. The landscape represents the aspects of self. This is the image of "inner bridges".

Kyanite is a powerful and beautiful stone that forms in blade-like crystals and massive form, exhibiting a beautiful silvery blue to green color. Kyanite initiates psychic ability and promotes communication with higher beings. It is a stone whose physical structure and vibration make it a wonderful transmitter of energy from one being to another. It can therefore be used to enhance telepathy between two persons, and to transmit energy from healing facilitator to client.

Kyanite is one of the most prominent Allies to be used for Crystal Resonance Therapy™ and healing. It can clear the energetic field of a person and create a protective shield that will provide a safe space in which to do psychic or healing work. Kyanite's frequency mandates one to act upon intuitive guidance. It is in this manner that we build strong bridges between our inner and outer selves.

Kyanite's frequency facilitates the creation of inner bridges. These bridges are spans of energy between one person and another, oneself and one's higher self, or oneself and the world. It is these bridges that we use when we wish to transmit our true energy to another, or to receive true impressions from another.

Kyanite's ability to transmit and transport energy enables it to easily create and discreate these inner bridges. It's protective qualities enable it to keep guard against misuse by oneself or another in sending or receiving energy. Kyanite's key word is connection. It is through the building of these inner bridges that true connection and interconnection occurs.

In the coming Age of Light on Earth, we will be using our innate abilities of subtle perception more frequently. Through the building of bridges between one mind and another, we facilitate the process of true interaction– as one energy being to another. Our understanding and acceptance of others becomes more complete, allowing us to share our own higher energy with those who may require support.

Kyanite is the Ally that will aid us in opening these inner doorways between our true selves. Call upon the energy of Kyanite to aid you in creating bridges of energy between your physical and non-physical selves. This is the first step toward healing the illusion of separation that we have created, and manifesting the Age of Light on the Earth plane.

THE MESSAGES

Kyanite has come to you to aid you in making those inner and outer connections that are necessary for your development. Perhaps a new relationship or opportunity is moving your way which will aid you on your path. Or perhaps you are being asked to "make the connection" between disparate aspects of your life.

All events and circumstances in our lives are a silent dance that the Universe orchestrates for our highest good. Every coincidence or happenstance is actually a carefully planned event that connects you to your next level of learning. Beneath every event and circumstance is the hand of the Divine, co-creating with you in your life.

Kyanite is sending you a message that the obstacles that you see on your path will soon be overcome. New bridges will be built that will carry you over difficulty, and will allow you to perceive your connection to the Divine.

CHAKRA: Sixth and Crown
AFFIRMATION: The Universe is working
to connect me with my highest good.

PRAYER

(FULGURITE)

Fulgurite

PRAYER

In this image, the diverse energies of spirit are focused into a powerful beam of communication to the Divine. Through this beam, gifts are sent from the Divine to the Earth plane, manifesting light upon the planet. This is the image of prayer, which is a state of equal exchange of energies between the Universe and self. This is the energy of Fulgurite.

Fulgurites are hollow, tubelike formations that are not true crystals. Fulgurites are created by lightning striking sand with such energy that the sand is melted into a type of natural glass. Because of the incredible energy inherent in the lightning's merging with the sand, Fulgurites are the most powerful of Allies to call upon for Storm energy.

The hollow tube of the Fulgurite acts as an amplification chamber for the energies that are constantly being released from the lightning fused glass. This hollow tube can be used as a type of prayer pipe, with the user blowing their prayer through the tube, and releasing it to the Universe.

When we pray, our breath, mixed with our intention, thanksgiving, and blessings, are sent to the heavens. The Storm element carries our prayers to the Universe on Wind, cleanses our souls with Water, transforms us with the light of Fire, and manifests our prayers on Earth. For this reason, Storm is the most potent Ally to call upon when your prayers need added strength.

Fulgurites carry the power of storm. By invoking Fulgurite's powerful Storm energy, we can enhance our prayers' effectiveness and speed them on their way to the Universe. Because of their origin in the union of Sky and Earth at the moment of Storm, Fulgurites carry the energy of both the spirit world and the physical world. With this fusion of energies, Fulgurite can be used as a link between the physical and non-physical realms.

Fulgurite can be used on any of the chakras, clearing and exposing the blockages and lessons of each. Like the element of Storm, Fulgurite's energy is intense, creating a deep movement of energy that clears all debris from one's life.

THE MESSAGE

Fulgurite is speaking to you of the power of prayer to create radical and unforeseeable change in your life. Fulgurite is ready to carry your prayers and wishes to the Universe, but don't expect them to manifest in any usual way. The Universe is on the verge of supplying you with a new and totally different direction.

The old saying, "Be careful what you pray for, for you will surely get it," is certainly true in this case. That which you have been praying for is about to be manifested! Expect the Universe to throw in a couple of lessons along with the gift, however, and give thanks for all that you are about to learn.

Just as the Storm brings renewal and rebirth, so too does the energy of Fulgurite. Embrace it's vibration and open yourself to it's frequency. You will soon understand that when you are centered in prayers of thanksgiving and surrender to the Divine, all of your true desires will be answered.

CHAKRA: All

AFFIRMATION: I am thankful for the blessings
that are manifest in my life.

Azeztulite

Alternate Realities

An ancient Mayan temple (mother ship?) is partially submerged in the ocean. Smaller ships gather to refuel on the energy that the temple supplies. Probably not something that you would see on a trip to Mexico, but does that mean that it is not real? Our perception of reality is limited by our beliefs and the development of our extrasensory perception. Though this image is not 'real', it does represent the concept of "alternate realities", which are those realities that are open to our minds, if not our senses. The realm of alternate realities is governed by the Ally Azeztulite.

Azeztulite is a form of Quartz that has been etherically programmed by interdimensional beings to carry the energy of the Great Central Sun of our Universe. This stone has a fine, high vibration. To date, it has only been found in one location in the southeastern United States, and was first thought to be a form of Phenacite because of both the location in which it was found, and the energy of the stone itself. Azeztulite looks quite a bit like broken glass, and can be faceted into a beautiful clear gemstone.

Azeztulite speaks to us of alternate realities. As humans, we inhabit a very narrow range of reality. It is as though we walk this Earth with blinders on, never seeing the incredible depth and beauty of all of the levels of reality that surround us. Azeztulite was sent as an Ally that can aid us in connecting with the other realms that surround us, and enable us to open to the true scope of perception that we are capable of.

The coming Age of Light is about opening ourselves to these other, more expanded, levels of reality. It is about reconnecting with the source of energy that exists beyond us all, and is embodied in the Great Central Sun of this Universe. Azeztulite carries this energy, and when we resonate with it, it shares this broadened prospective with us.

Opening to the alternate realities of the plant world, mineral world and animal world are the first steps toward reclaiming our Earth and healing ourselves and the paradise planet that we were given to live upon. Opening to the alternate realities of the Light beings and subtle energy beings is another connection that must be made if we are to survive on this planet in physical form.

Azeztulite has come to aid us in perceiving and connecting with all of these levels that exist around us. From this connection we will gain a greater wisdom and understanding of the beings that we truly are– beings of Light.

THE MESSAGE

Azeztulite is calling you to let go of any and all densities in your life, and embrace the higher energies that are waiting to move through you. This is the card of the priesthood, in that it heralds in a time of dedication to service in the Light, especially in the realms of bringing through new ways to live, give, and survive.

Azeztulite has come to aid you in perceiving the many levels of reality that surround you. Through the exploration of these realities, you can gain the insight and understanding necessary to manifest your purpose on Earth. Open yourself to the kingdoms of Earth, the Light beings of the spiritual realms, and to your own self. This Ally has come to facilitate your awakening to your true self, and your place in the web of Light that surrounds you.

Be aware of subtle impressions, dreams, feelings, or other indicators that a message is being sent to you from other levels of reality. It may be that you are being prepared for contact by beings from another realm. In the coming times, we will need to rely upon these messages in order to survive. Open yourself now to the signals and messages of these realms, so that you can become a voice for these beings in the coming times.

CHAKRA: Third eye, Crown and etheric
AFFIRMATION: I perceive my reality
in the Light of the Divine.

P HENACITE

INITIATION

In this image, human spirit approaches the Phenacite doorway– the entrance to the higher realms. The being is prepared for her initiation into the new ways of thinking and living that are revealed when one integrates one's Light body into the physical vehicle. Phenacite is the Ally that embodies this frequency of initiation into new levels of being.

Phenacite is a rare beryllium silicate that forms into wand-like crystals (Madagascar and Namibia) and rhomboidal, disk-like crystals (Russian, Brazilian, and Colorado). It can range in color from golden to colorless to gray. Phenacite is one of the Storm Element Allies, because of it's transformative and enlightening effect upon the human energy field. When awakened and employed as an Ally, this stone will initiate the Light body, and aid in grounding it into the physical plane.

Phenacite's key word is initiation. Most cultures have initiation ceremonies that provide their people with definite rites of passage. These rites give the initiate an opportunity to eradicate outmoded aspects of their lives, and to begin the new. Through the rites of birth, puberty, partnering, croning and death, people were able to explore the spiritual meaning of these stages of their lives. The rites of passage act as 'signposts' by which one can steer one's life.

In ancient times, dedicating one's life to Spirit was also done through initiation. One would declare one's intent before a teacher or spiritual mentor, and would receive an initiation into the teachings of that society. As a student progressed, new initiations would be given in order to allow the student to rededicate herself to the spiritual path. These initiations were often accompanied by the revelation of spiritual knowledge that would take the student to the next level. In this way, the student would gain new levels of growth and understanding.

Today, our emerging system of spiritual growth is much more eclectic and personally directed than in the past. Spiritual seekers often study alone, or with many different teachers, in order to gain the knowledge they seek. This can sometimes be difficult, because of the lack of initiatory experiences that clearly delineate the growth of the student to new levels of being. Phenacite is an Ally that has appeared in this New Age of Light in order to initiate the Lightworker to ever higher levels of awareness.

THE MESSAGE

When Phenacite appears in your cards, you can be sure that an initiatory experience will soon follow. There may be a new guide coming into your life, or perhaps there is a rite of passage ahead that will be an opportunity for deep growth. Phenacite is signaling you that the time of Storm is approaching. You will be tested by the elements of your life, and you may be asked to sacrifice those things that are keeping you from moving forward.

This Ally signals the time of awakening, of changing from chrysalis to butterfly. You can no longer claim the ignorance of a child when answering for your creations. You are being asked to take responsibility as an adult for all that you are experiencing, and in so doing, acknowledge your own power to create the life you are destined for. Now is the time to invoke the energy of Phenacite in preparation for your initiation into the new role that the Universe has in store for you.

CHAKRA: Third eye and Crown chakras
AFFIRMATION: I dedicate myself
to the path of the spiritual initiate.

Bibliography

Bentov, Itzhak. Stalking the Wild Pendulum: On the Mechanics of
     Consciousness. Rochester: Destiny, 1977

Smith, M.D., Fritz Frederick. Inner Bridges: A Guide to Energy Movement and
     Body Structure. Atlanta: Humanics, 1987

Simmons, Robert & Kathy Warner. Moldavite:Starborn Stone of Transformation.
     Gloucester: Heaven & Earth Books, 1988

Brennan, Barbara Ann. Hands of Light: A Guide to Healing Through the Human
     Energy Field. New York: Bantam, 1988

Brennan, Barbara Ann. Light Emerging: The Journey of Personal Healing.
     New York: Bantam, 1993

Raphaell, Katrina. Crystal Enlightenment.
     Taos: Aurora, 1985

Raphaell, Katrina. Crystal Healing.
     Taos: Aurora, 1986

Raphaell, Katrina. Crystalline Transmission.
     Taos: Aurora, 1987

Melody. Love Is In The Earth: A Kaleidoscope of Crystals .
     Wheat Ridge: Earth-Love, 1995

ABOUT THE AUTHOR

Psychically open since birth, Naisha has been aware of the power and healing potential of crystals and stones since she was a child. Incarnating on the path of the wounded healer, Naisha's difficult childhood led her to deeply explore the spiritual side of nature and humanity. This exploration led her down the path of personal healing and, eventually, allowed her to aid others on their own healing path.

Classically trained in various bodywork modalities, Naisha is the creator of Crystal Resonance Therapy™. This system of vibrational medicine employs crystals, natural elemental forces, and other vibrational sources for inner exploration, healing, and spiritual growth. She is also the founder of the Crystalis Institute, offering CRT training and personal healing retreats.

Naisha has worked with thousands of people worldwide as a healer and as a consultant on the properties of gemstones and crystals.

For more information on Crystal Resonance Therapy™ Cerification Training, personal readings with Naisha, workshops and other programs, please contact:

Crystalis Institute
P.O. Box 827
Hardwick, VT 05843-0827 USA
Toll Free (U.S. & Canada) 866-462-4742 (866-4-NAISHA)
Outside the U.S. & Canada 802-472-5511
URL: www.crystalisinstitute.com
email: info@crystalisinstitute.com

About Heaven & Earth

Heaven and Earth Publishing LLC has been publishing books since 1989. Its sister company Heaven and Earth Jewelry, established in 1986, specializes in Metaphysical Jewelry, Minerals and Gems, and offers a FREE Color Catalog with over 2000 items, including all the stones in the Crystal Ally Cards.
Call or email for your FREE Catalog,
1-800-942-9423
email: heavenandearth@earthlink.net
or visit our website at
heavenandearthjewelry.com

Heaven & Earth LLC
POB 249
East Montpelier, VT 05651

For those who enjoy working with the Crystal Ally Cards, a further dimension of possibility can be opened by working with the cards in conjunction with the stones themselves. We offer below a price list for each of the stones featured in *The Crystal Ally Cards*. They can be ordered, either singly or as a set, directly from Heaven & Earth. The stones offered here are generally the least expensive version of the particular stone. (i.e. Most of the $1 stones are tumbled.) For information on these, call or write with your questions. Our order line is 800-942-9423 (U.S. & Canada) or 802-476-4775. Email us at heavenandearth@earthlink.net or write to Heaven & Earth LLC, PO Box 249, East Montpelier, VT 05651, USA.

Amazonite $1
Amethyst $1
Aquamarine $2
Aventurine $1
Azeztulite $5
Azurite $3
Black Tourmaline $5
Bloodstone $1
Calcite $1
Carnelian $1
Chlorite $20
Citrine $1
Charoite $5
Chrysocolla $2
Clear Quartz $1
Cuprite $10
Danburite $5
Dioptase $10
Fluorite $1
Fulgurite $5
Garnet $1
Golden Topaz $10
Hematite $1
Herderite $15
Kunzite & Hiddenite $10
Kyanite $5
Labradorite $5
Lapis Lazuli $6
Larimar $5
Lepidolite $2

Malachite $1
Moldavite $10
Moonstone $1
Obsidian $1
Petrified Wood $1
Phenacite $20
Pyrite $5
Rhodocrosite $2
Rhodonite $1
Rose Quartz $1
Ruby $5
Selenite $5
Smokey Quartz $1
Sodalite $1
Sugilite $5
Sunstone $5
Tiger Eye $1
Tourmaline $5
Turquoise $3
Zincite $10.
Total: $225
Special price for entire set $200

Also Available
Additional Copies of
The Crystal Ally Cards **$29.95 ea.**

NOTES